Great Britain:
Past and Present

A multicultural society with a colonial past

Contents

Module I Pre-reading activities

Part A Colonialism and multiculturalism in Great Britain   4
  A1 Working with words   4
  A2 Multicultural Britain: then and now   5
  A3 Post-colonial debates   5

Module II While-reading activities

Part A Shooting an Elephant   8
  A1 'Shooting an Elephant' *George Orwell*   8
  A2 Working for the Empire   16
  A3 The pressure to act   18
  A4 Reflecting on colonialism   19

Part B My Son the Fanatic   20
  B1 'My Son the Fanatic' *Hanif Kureishi*   20
  B2 Diversity in the UK   33

Part C The Embassy of Cambodia   34
  C1 'The Embassy of Cambodia' *Zadie Smith*   34
  C2 A migration journey   52
  C3 'New Person and Old Person'   53
  C4 The turning point   54
  C5 Modern slavery?   56

Module III Post-reading activities

Part A Reviewing colonial and post-colonial challenges   58
  A1 A colonial experience: 'An Outpost for Progress' *Joseph Conrad*   58
  A2 The London bombings on 7 July 2005   61
  A3 A multicultural experience: 'A Pair of Jeans' *Qaisra Shahraz*   63

Acknowledgements   Inner back cover

Info boxes (in alphabetical order)

George Orwell 16
Hanif Kureishi 30
Language 32
Modern slavery 57
Narrators and narrations 54
Zadie Smith 52

Abbreviations and symbols

adj	adjective
AE	American English
BE	British English
cf.	compare
f./ff.	and the following page(s)/line(s)
fml	formal
infml	informal
jdm., jdn.	*jemandem, jemanden*
l., ll.	line, lines
n	noun
p., pp.	page, pages
pl	plural
sb.	somebody
sl	slang
sth.	something
usu.	usually
v	verb

📄⊙ **cornelsen.de**
+◁) **Code: xxxxx**

The webcode(s) can be entered at www.cornelsen.de to connect you directly to the website you want.

▶⊕ Viewing task (video available)

Pre-reading activities

Part A
Colonialism and multiculturalism in Great Britain

A1 Working with words

1 Look at the word banks below and on the next page. Make sure you understand all the words. If necessary, check the meanings in a dictionary.

Word bank colonialism

colonialism · colonize sth. · the colonized · empire · conquer sth. · defeat sb./sth. · slavery · indigenous · exploitation · economy · infrastructure · trade · tariff · natural resource · influence sb./sth. · power · rule sth. · military · superior · inferior · administration · impose taxes · advantage · disadvantage · labour · impact (on) sb./sth. · develop (into sth.) · shape sb./sth. · cultural identity · rebellion · independence · establish sth. · determine sth. · serve sb./sth. · innovation · supremacy · paternalistic · marginalization · uprising · native · political ties · hostility · settle sth./somewhere

Word bank multiculturalism

multiculturalism · integrate sb. (into/with sth.) · integration · inclusion · cultural appropriation · assimilation · adopt sth. · tension · discriminate against sth./sb. · racism · community · migration · immigrant · emigrant · asylum seeker · citizenship · tolerance · enrichment · (ethnic) minority · diversity · melting pot · globalization · border crossing · deport sb. · deportation · inequality · (upward) social mobility · extremism · liberalism · enforce sth. · enable sth./sb. · freedom of speech · endorse sth./sb. · promote sth./sb. · feel welcome · tackle a challenge · rootless · segregated communities · social investment · contribute (to) sth. · prosperity · cultural identity · resentment · encourage sb./sth.

2 Work with a partner and complete tasks **a** and **b**. Try to use as many of the words from the boxes as possible.
   a What do you already know about colonialism and its impact on both colonizers and indigenous populations?
   b Discuss some of the challenges immigrants may encounter when they settle in a country that has different cultural traditions from their home country.

A2 Multicultural Britain: then and now

1 **a** Form four groups. Each group will be assigned one of the following topics.
   A The British Empire and its legacy
   B The Commonwealth of Nations
   C Multicultural Britain
   D Brexit and the immigration debate
   b Prepare a short presentation on the topic you have been assigned.
   c Speaking Give your presentation. Take short notes during the other groups' presentations.

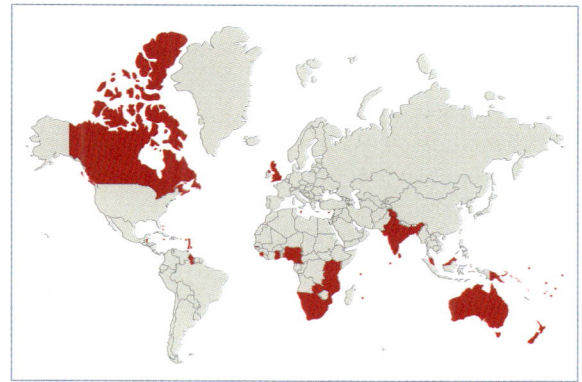

Members of the British Commonwealth of Nations

A3 Post-colonial debates

1 Mediation You have been partnered with a student in Canada to work on a visual project about colonialism. Your teacher has provided the interview on pp. 6–7 to get started on the subject. Your Canadian partner, however, does not speak German. Write her an email in which you summarize Dr. Shashi Tharoor's view of colonial and post-colonial India.

Ein Kniefall der Vergebung *Krisha Kops*

**In seinem Buch *An Era of Darkness: The British Empire in India*
kritisiert der Politiker und Autor Dr. Shashi Tharoor die britische
Kolonialherrschaft und ihre Verteidiger. Wir haben ihn dazu befragt.**

*A silver coin from the
Indian British colonial era,
1941*

*Dr. Tharoor, Sie fordern, dass jemand wie Prince Charles nach dem
Vorbild von Willy Brandt in Warschau in Amritsar niederknien sollte,
um sich für die britische Kolonialherrschaft in Indien zu entschuldigen.
Warum diese Forderung?*

5   Weil das Massaker von Jallianwala Bagh in vielerlei Hinsicht
symptomatisch für die schlimmsten Gräuel in British-Indien ist: 200
Jahre voller Ausbeutung, Plünderungen, Beutezüge, Diebstahl, Morde
und erzwungene Hungersnöte, in denen Menschen umkamen. In
Jallianwala Bagh fragte Colonel Reginald Dyer die Demonstranten
10 nicht nach ihren Forderungen, verlangte nicht, die Demonstration
aufzulösen und sich zu zerstreuen, ließ noch nicht einmal Warnschüsse
abgeben … er befahl den Truppen einfach, das Feuer auf wehrlose
Männer, Frauen und Kinder zu eröffnen. 1379 Menschen starben,
zahllose weitere wurde zum Teil schwer verletzt. Wenn sich der Tag am
15 13. April 2019 zum hundertsten Mal jährt, hätte es angesichts noch
immer offener Wunden heilsame Effekte und könnte einiges an Schuld
tilgen, wenn jemand – idealerweise ein Mitglied der königlichen
Familie – nach Amritsar kommen und auf die Knie fallen würde.

Sie geben Britisch-Indien nicht nur die Schuld an den Gräueltaten, sondern
20 *bezichtigen die ehemalige Kolonialherrschaft auch, die Grundlage für
heutige Konflikte wie jenen zwischen Hindus und Muslimen geschaffen
zu haben.*

   Die Politik des *divide et impera* geht zurück bis zur so genannten
Meuterei, dem Aufstand von 1857–58, als indische Soldaten – Hindus
25 und Muslime gemeinsam – gegen die britischen Lords aufstanden und
Seite an Seite dafür kämpften, die Kolonialherrschaft zu beenden. Die
Briten unterdrückten diese Bestrebungen mit größter Härte, in Delhi
allein wurden 100 000 Menschen getötet. Die Briten schworen, dass sich
dies niemals wiederholen werde. Die geeignetste Maßnahme bestand
30 darin, die Inder gegeneinander aufzubringen. Dieser Strategie folgte
man und schaffte so ein jeweils eigenes Bewusstsein bei Muslimen und
Hindus. Wie durch die Schaffung der Muslim League als Gegenbewegung
zum Indian National Congress, der 1885 gegründet worden war, oder
durch die britische Teilung von Bengalen im Jahr 1905.

35 *Die führte dann ironischerweise zu etwas für die Briten Unerwünschtem …*

   Genau. Diese agitatorische Konstruktion von Bewusstsein gewann
an Eigendynamik und führte zu der beklagenswerten Teilung des
Landes in Indien und Pakistan, d. h. mündete in der Teilung von 1947.

Die Bestrebungen der Briten hatten letztlich zur Folge, dass Indien
40 nicht mehr als ein ganzes Land zu regieren war. [...]

*Gehören nicht auch Erfolge zu den Hinterlassenschaften der britischen
Herrschaft? Das Bahnsystem beispielsweise?*

Es gibt eine Reihe von positiven Hinterlassenschaften, allerdings
keine, die tatsächlich wirklich Indien hätten zu Gute kommen sollen.
45 Die Bahnlinien waren Teil des kolonialen Betrugs. Das Bahnnetz war
für die Briten ein äußerst profitables Unternehmen. Die Infrastruktur
wurde komplett aus indischen Steuereinnahmen bezahlt, die Gewinne
flossen komplett in die Taschen der britischen Investoren. Die
Bahnlinien wurden gebaut, um Bodenschätze aus dem Inneren Indiens
50 in die Hafenstädte zu bringen, von wo sie nach England verschifft
wurden. Oder um Truppen verlegen zu können, wenn Aufstände
drohten. Mit anderen Worten, ganz gleich, ob es sich um die Eisenbahn,
die Gesetzgebung, die englische Sprache oder natürlich auch um das
Bildungssystem handelt, alle diese Einrichtungen waren Werkzeuge
55 zur Unterstützung der britischen Herrschaft, der Ausdehnung der
britischen Interessen und Steigerung britischer Profite. [...]

*Train from Shimla to
Kalka in India*

Wie sollte Indien Ihrer Meinung nach in 70 Jahren aussehen?

Mehr als alles andere muss sich Indien um seine Armen kümmern.
Ob wir nun um 9% (während meiner Regierungszeit) oder um 6%
60 (unter der derzeitigen Regierung) wachsen, ist letztlich einerlei. Was
zählt sind die 25% ganz unten in der Gesellschaftspyramide. Wenn
wir nicht sicherstellen können, dass jeder im Land drei ordentliche
Mahlzeiten pro Tag bekommt, ein Dach über dem Kopf, Bildung,
eine gute Gesundheitsversorgung und Aussicht auf ein besseres
65 Leben hat, dann haben wir gesellschaftlich versagt. Das bedeutet,
wir sollten all unsere anderen Großprojekte zurückstellen – wie das
Raumfahrtprogramm oder IT. Es gab eine Zeit – und die liegt länger
zurück –, da war Indien das erfolgreichste Land der Welt. Ich will
damit nicht sagen, dass wir dahin zurückkehren können. Die Welt ist
70 heutzutage eine gerechtere. Gott sei Dank! Aber es könnte uns besser
gehen, als es uns heute geht. Dafür müssen wir arbeiten.

*From: Krisha Kops,
„Ein Kniefall der
Vergebung", Online:
https://www.goethe.de/
ins/in/de/kul/mag/
21168773.html –
Copyright: © Goethe-
Institut/Max Mueller
Bhavan New Delhi
Februar 2018*

2 Form groups of 3 to 5 students. Discuss whether you support
Dr. Tharoor's demand that Prince Charles should apologize for
Britain's colonial rule in India.

Language Help
on the one hand, ... • on the other hand, ... • I fully support ... • I strongly disagree •
I would recommend ... • In my view ... • First of all ... • For this reason ... • absolutely •
We mustn't forget ... • That's probably true, but... • To illustrate this point ... • There is
strong evidence that ... • So, if I understand you correctly, ...

While-reading activities

Part A

Shooting an Elephant

A1 **Shooting an Elephant** *George Orwell*

In his essay 'Shooting an Elephant', first published in 1936, George Orwell reflects on his life as an official of the British colonial administration in Burma. He explores the conflict of fulfilling his duties while facing the local population's hatred of the colonial government. When he is called to deal with an elephant that has gone out of control, he is torn between his own judgement and the expectations the native population has of him. Read the text and complete the tasks that follow on pp. 16–19.

In Moulmein, in Lower Burma, I was hated by large numbers of people
– the only time in my life that I have been important enough for this
to happen to me. I was sub-divisional police officer of the town, and
in an aimless, petty kind of way anti-European feeling was very bitter.
5 No one had the guts to raise a riot, but if a European woman went
through the bazaars alone somebody would probably spit betel juice
over her dress. As a police officer I was an obvious target and was
baited whenever it seemed safe to do so. When a nimble Burman
tripped me up on the football field and the referee (another Burman)
10 looked the other way, the crowd yelled with hideous laughter. This
happened more than once. In the end the sneering yellow faces of
young men that met me everywhere, the insults hooted after me when
I was at a safe distance, got badly on my nerves. The young Buddhist
priests were the worst of all. There were several thousands of them
15 in the town and none of them seemed to have anything to do except
stand on street corners and jeer at Europeans.

All this was perplexing and upsetting. For at that time I had already
made up my mind that imperialism was an evil thing and the sooner
I chucked up my job and got out of it the better. Theoretically – and
20 secretly, of course – I was all for the Burmese and all against their
oppressors, the British. As for the job I was doing, I hated it more
bitterly than I can perhaps make clear. In a job like that you see
the dirty work of Empire at close quarters. The wretched prisoners
huddling in the stinking cages of the lock-ups, the grey, cowed faces of
25 the long-term convicts, the scarred buttocks of the men who had been
flogged with bamboos – all these oppressed me with an intolerable
sense of guilt. But I could get nothing into perspective. I was young
and ill-educated and I had had to think out my problems in the utter
silence that is imposed on every Englishman in the East. I did not even
30 know that the British Empire is dying, still less did I know that it is a
great deal better than the younger empires that are going to supplant
it. All I knew was that I was stuck between my hatred of the empire I
served and my rage against the evil-spirited little beasts who tried to
make my job impossible. With one part of my mind I thought of the
35 British Raj as an unbreakable tyranny, as something clamped down,
in saecula saeculorum, upon the will of prostrate peoples; with another
part I thought that the greatest joy in the world would be to drive a
bayonet into a Buddhist priest's guts. Feelings like these are the normal
by-products of imperialism; ask any Anglo-Indian official, if you can
40 catch him off duty.

One day something happened which in a roundabout way was
enlightening. It was a tiny incident in itself, but it gave me a better
glimpse than I had had before of the real nature of imperialism – the
real motives for which despotic governments act. Early one morning
45 the sub-inspector at a police station the other end of town rang me

[1] **Moulmein** city in Burma (now known as Mawlamyine)
[3] **sub-divisional** of a low rank
[4] **petty** *kleinlich*
[5] **have the guts to do sth.** (infml) have the courage to do sth.
[6] **betel** ['bi:tl] Asian palm tree (parts of which are chewed for their intoxicating effect)
[8] **bait sb.** (here) torment sb., tease sb.
nimble agile and skilful
[10] **hideous** ['hɪdiəs] horrible
[11] **sneer at sb./sth.** (v) show you have no respect for sb./sth. through a facial expression
[12] **hoot** (v) yell, shout
[16] **jeer at sb.** make fun of sb.
[19] **chuck sth. up** (infml) quit sth.
[23] **at close quarters** from close up
[24] **huddle** (v) *kauern*
lock-up (n) prison
cowed [kaʊd] frightened
[31] **supplant sb./sth.** replace sb./sth.
[35] **British Raj** [rɑːdʒ] British government of India
clamp down *rigoros durchgreifen*
[36] **in saecula saeculorum** (Latin) forever
prostrate (adj, fml) (here) oppressed, defeated
[44] **despotic** tyrannical

A Burmese bazaar

up on the phone and said that an elephant was ravaging the bazaar. Would I please come and do something about it? I did not know what I could do, but I wanted to see what was happening and I got on to a pony and started out. I took my rifle, an old .44 Winchester and much
50 too small to kill an elephant, but I thought the noise might be useful *in terrorem*. Various Burmans stopped me on the way and told me about the elephant's doings. It was not, of course, a wild elephant, but a tame one which had gone 'must'. It had been chained up, as tame elephants always are when their attack of 'must' is due, but on the previous night it had broken its chain and escaped. Its mahout, the
55 only person who could manage it when it was in that state, had set out in pursuit, but had taken the wrong direction and was now twelve hours' journey away, and in the morning the elephant had suddenly reappeared in the town. The Burmese population had no weapons and were quite helpless against it. It had already destroyed somebody's
60 bamboo hut, killed a cow, and raided some fruit-stalls and devoured the stock; also it had met the municipal rubbish van and, when the driver jumped out and took to his heels, had turned the van over and inflicted violence upon it.

The Burmese sub-inspector and some Indian constables were
65 waiting for me in the quarter where the elephant had been seen. It was a very poor quarter, a labyrinth of squalid bamboo huts, thatched with palm-leaf, winding all over a steep hillside. I remember that it was a cloudy, stuffy morning at the beginning of the rains. We began questioning the people as to where the elephant had gone and, as
70 usual, failed to get any definite information. That is invariably the case

46 **ravage sth.** [ˈrævɪdʒ] destroy sth.
51 **in terrorem** (Latin) as a threat
53 **must/musth** (n) (here) period when male elephants go mad in search of a female elephant to mate with
54 **mahout** [məˈhaʊt] elephant keeper or trainer
61 **municipal** *kommunal*
64 **constable** [ˈkʌnstəbl] police officer
66 **squalid** in bad condition
thatch sth. with sth. cover sth. (usu. a roof) with sth.

in the East; a story always sounds clear enough at a distance, but the
nearer you get to the scene of events the vaguer it becomes. Some of
the people said that the elephant had gone in one direction, some said
that he had gone in another, some professed not even to have heard of
75   any elephant. I had almost made up my mind that the whole story was
a pack of lies, when we heard yells a little distance away. There was a
loud, scandalized cry of 'Go away, child! Go away this instant!' and an
old woman with a switch in her hand came round the corner of a hut,
violently shooing away a crowd of naked children. Some more women
80   followed, clicking their tongues and exclaiming; evidently there was
something that the children ought not to have seen. I rounded the hut
and saw a man's dead body sprawling in the mud. He was an Indian, a
black Dravidian coolie, almost naked, and he could not have been dead
many minutes. The people said that the elephant had come suddenly
85   upon him round the corner of the hut, caught him with its trunk, put
its foot on his back, and ground him into the earth. This was the rainy
season and the ground was soft, and his face had scored a trench a foot
deep and a couple of yards long. He was lying on his belly with arms
crucified and head sharply twisted to one side. His face was coated
90   with mud, the eyes wide open, the teeth bared and grinning with an
expression of unendurable agony. (Never tell me, by the way, that the
dead look peaceful. Most of the corpses I have seen looked devilish.)
The friction of the great beast's foot had stripped the skin from his
back as neatly as one skins a rabbit. As soon as I saw the dead man I
95   sent an orderly to a friend's house nearby to borrow an elephant rifle.
I had already sent back the pony, not wanting it to go mad with fright
and throw me if it smelt the elephant.

   The orderly came back in a few minutes with a rifle and five
cartridges, and meanwhile some Burmans had arrived and told us that
100   the elephant was in the paddy fields below, only a few hundred yards
away. As I started forward practically the whole population of the
quarter flocked out of the houses and followed me. They had seen
the rifle and were all shouting excitedly that I was going to shoot the
elephant. They had not shown much interest in the elephant when
105   he was merely ravaging their homes, but it was different now that
he was going to be shot. It was a bit of fun to them, as it would be to
an English crowd; besides they wanted the meat. It made me vaguely
uneasy. I had no intention of shooting the elephant – I had merely sent
for the rifle to defend myself if necessary – and it is always unnerving
110   to have a crowd following you. I marched down the hill, looking and
feeling a fool, with the rifle over my shoulder and an ever-growing
army of people jostling at my heels. At the bottom, when you got away
from the huts, there was a metalled road and beyond that a miry waste
of paddy fields a thousand yards across, not yet ploughed but soggy
115   from the first rains and dotted with coarse grass. The elephant was

[78] **switch** (n) rod, stick
[82] **sprawl** (v) (here) lie
   stretched out
[83] **Dravidian** (adj)
   belonging to a people
   from southern India
   and Sri Lanka
   coolie unskilled
   labourer
[85] **trunk** (here) an elephant's nose
[86] **grind sb./sth. (ground
   – ground)** (hier) jdn./
   etwas zermalmen
[87] **score a trench** (here)
   make a hole
[90] **bare your teeth** show
   your teeth
[93] **friction** Reibung
[99] **cartridge** Patrone
[100] **paddy field** field in
   which rice is grown
[102] **flock out** come out in
   crowds
[109] **unnerve sb.** make sb.
   nervous, frighten sb.
[112] **jostle at sb./sth.**
   crowd around sb./sth.
[113] **metalled road**
   Schotterstraße
   miry ['maɪəri] muddy
   or swampy
[114] **plough sth.** [plaʊ]
   etwas pflügen
   soggy wet
[115] **coarse** [kɔːs] rough

standing eight yards from the road, his left side towards us. He took not the slightest notice of the crowd's approach. He was tearing up bunches of grass, beating them against his knees to clean them and stuffing them into his mouth.

120   I had halted on the road. As soon as I saw the elephant I knew with perfect certainty that I ought not to shoot him. It is a serious matter to shoot a working elephant – it is comparable to destroying a huge and costly piece of machinery – and obviously one ought not to do it if it can possibly be avoided. And at that distance, peacefully eating, the
125 elephant looked no more dangerous than a cow. I thought then and I think now that his attack of 'must' was already passing off; in which case he would merely wander harmlessly about until the mahout came back and caught him. Moreover, I did not in the least want to shoot him. I decided that I would watch him for a little while to make sure
130 that he did not turn savage again, and then go home.

    But at that moment, I glanced round at the crowd that had followed me. It was an immense crowd, two thousand at the least and growing every minute. It blocked the road for a long distance on either side. I looked at the sea of yellow faces above the garish clothes – faces all
135 happy and excited over this bit of fun, all certain that the elephant was going to be shot. They were watching me as they would watch a conjuror about to perform a trick. They did not like me, but with the magical rifle in my hands I was momentarily worth watching. And suddenly I realized that I should have to shoot the elephant after all.
140 The people expected it of me and I had got to do it; I could feel their two thousand wills pressing me forward, irresistibly. And it was at this moment, as I stood there with the rifle in my hands, that I first grasped the hollowness, the futility of the white man's dominion in the East. Here was I, the white man with his gun, standing in front of the
145 unarmed native crowd – seemingly the leading actor of the piece; but in reality I was only an absurd puppet pushed to and fro by the will of those yellow faces behind. I perceived in this moment that when the white man turns tyrant it is his own freedom that he destroys. He becomes a sort of hollow, posing dummy, the conventionalized figure
150 of a sahib. For it is the condition of his rule that he shall spend his life in trying to impress the 'natives', and so in every crisis he has got to do what the 'natives' expect of him. He wears a mask, and his face grows to fit it. I had got to shoot the elephant. I had committed myself to doing it when I sent for the rifle. A sahib has got to act like
155 a sahib; he has got to appear resolute, to know his own mind and do definite things. To come all that way, rifle in hand, with two thousand people marching at my heels, and then to trail feebly away, having done nothing – no, that was impossible. The crowd would laugh at me. And my whole life, every white man's life in the East, was one long
160 struggle not to be laughed at.

[134] **garish** strikingly colourful
[137] **conjuror** [ˈkʌndʒərə] magician
[143] **grasp sth.** understand sth.
[150] **sahib** (Urdu) European man of status
[157] **feeble** weak

But I did not want to shoot the elephant. I watched him beating his bunch of grass against his knees, with that preoccupied grandmotherly air that elephants have. It seemed to me that it would be murder to shoot him. At that age I was not squeamish about killing animals, but I had never shot an elephant and never wanted to. (Somehow it always seems worse to kill a *large* animal.) Besides, there was the beast's owner to be considered. Alive, the elephant was worth at least a hundred pounds; dead, he would only be worth the value of his tusks, five pounds, possibly. But I had got to act quickly. I turned to some experienced-looking Burmans who had been there when we arrived, and asked them how the elephant had been behaving. They all said the same thing: he took no notice of you if you left him alone, but he might charge if you went too close to him.

It was perfectly clear to me what I ought to do. I ought to walk up to within, say, twenty-five yards of the elephant and test his behaviour. If he charged, I could shoot; if he took no notice of me, it would be safe to leave him until the mahout came back. But also I knew that I was going to do no such thing. I was a poor shot with a rifle and the ground was soft mud into which one would sink at every step. If the elephant charged and I missed him, I should have about as much chance as a toad under a steam-roller. But even then I was not thinking particularly of my own skin, only of the watchful yellow faces behind. For at that moment, with the crowd watching me, I was not afraid in the ordinary sense, as I would have been if I had been alone. A white man mustn't be frightened in front of 'natives'; and so, in general, he isn't frightened. The sole thought in my mind was that if anything went wrong those two thousand Burmans would see me pursued, caught, trampled on, and reduced to a grinning corpse like that Indian up the hill. And if that happened it was quite probable that some of them

165
170
175
180
185

163 **air** (here) appearance, impression given by sb./sth.
164 **squeamish** *zimperlich*
168 **tusk** *Stoßzahn*
173 **charge** (v) attack
181 **toad** *Kröte*
steam-roller *Dampfwalze*

13

190 would laugh. That would never do. There was only one alternative. I shoved the cartridges into the magazine and lay down on the road to get a better aim.

The crowd grew very still, and a deep, low, happy sigh, as of people who see the theatre curtain go up at last, breathed from innumerable
195 throats. They were going to have their bit of fun after all. The rifle was a beautiful German thing with cross-hair sights. I did not then know that in shooting an elephant one should shoot to cut an imaginary bar running from ear-hole to ear-hole. I ought, therefore, as the elephant was sideways on, to have aimed straight at his ear-hole; actually
200 I aimed several inches in front of this, thinking the brain would be further forward.

When I pulled the trigger I did not hear the bang or feel the kick – one never does when a shot goes home – but I heard the devilish roar of glee that went up from the crowd. In that instant, in too short a time,
205 one would have thought, even for the bullet to get there, a mysterious, terrible change had come over the elephant. He neither stirred nor fell, but every line of his body had altered. He looked suddenly stricken, shrunken, immensely old, as though the frightful impact of the bullet had paralysed him without knocking him down.
210 At last, after what seemed a long time – it might have been five seconds, I dare say – he sagged flabbily to his knees. His mouth slobbered. An enormous senility seemed to have settled upon him. One could have imagined him thousands of years old. I fired again into the same spot. At the second shot he did not collapse but climbed
215 with desperate slowness to his feet and stood weakly upright, with legs sagging and head drooping. I fired a third time. That was the shot that did for him. You could see the agony of it jolt his whole body and knock the last remnant of strength from his legs. But in falling he seemed for a moment to rise, for as his hind legs collapsed beneath
220 him he seemed to tower upwards like a huge rock toppling, his trunk reaching skywards like a tree. He trumpeted, for the first and only time. And then down he came, his belly towards me, with a crash that seemed to shake the ground even where I lay.

I got up. The Burmans were already racing past me across the mud.
225 It was obvious that the elephant would never rise again, but he was not dead. He was breathing very rhythmically with long rattling gasps, his great mound of a side painfully rising and falling. His mouth was wide open. I could see far down into caverns of pale pink throat. I waited a long time for him to die, but his breathing did not weaken.
230 Finally, I fired my two remaining shots into the spot where I thought his heart must be. The thick blood welled out of him like red velvet, but still he did not die. His body did not even jerk when the shots hit him, the tortured breathing continued without a pause. He was dying, very slowly and in great agony, but in some world remote from me

191 **shove sth./sb.** [ʃʌv] push sth./sb.
196 **cross-hair sight** *Fadenkreuzvisier*
197 **bar** (n) (here) line
204 **glee** cheerfulness
206 **stir** (v) move
207 **alter** [ˈɔːltə] (v) change
211 **flabby** limp, slack
212 **slobber** *sabbern*
216 **droop** (v) hang down
217 **jolt sb./sth.** *etwas/ jdn. erschüttern*
218 **remnant** remains
226 **rattle** (v) *rasseln*
gasp (n) deep breath
227 **mound** heap
228 **cavern** [ˈkævən] *Höhle*
231 **velvet** type of soft cloth
232 **jerk** (v) move suddenly

235 where not even a bullet could damage him further. I felt I had got to put an end to that dreadful noise. It seemed dreadful to see the great beast lying there, powerless to move and yet powerless to die, and not even to be able to finish him. I sent back for my small rifle and poured shot after shot into his heart, and down his throat. They seemed to
240 make no impression. The tortured gasps continued as steadily as the ticking of a clock.

In the end I could not stand it any longer and went away. I heard later that it took him half an hour to die. Burmans were bringing dahs and baskets even before I left, and I was told they had stripped his
245 body almost to the bones by the afternoon.

Afterwards, of course, there were endless discussions about the shooting of the elephant. The owner was furious, but he was only an Indian and could do nothing. Besides, legally I had done the right thing, for a mad elephant has to be killed, like a mad dog, if its owner
250 fails to control it. Among the Europeans opinion was divided. The older men said I was right, the younger men said it was a damn shame to shoot an elephant for killing a coolie, because the elephant was worth more than any damn Coringhee coolie. And afterwards I was very glad that the coolie had been killed; it put me legally in the right and it gave
255 me a sufficient pretext for shooting the elephant. I often wondered whether any of the others grasped that I had done it solely to avoid looking a fool.

From: Orwell, Shooting an Elephant and Other Essays, *London: Penguin, 2003, pp. 31–40.*

243 **dah** (Burmese) knife
253 **Coringhee** [ˈkɒrɪŋgiː] people from southern India
255 **pretext** excuse

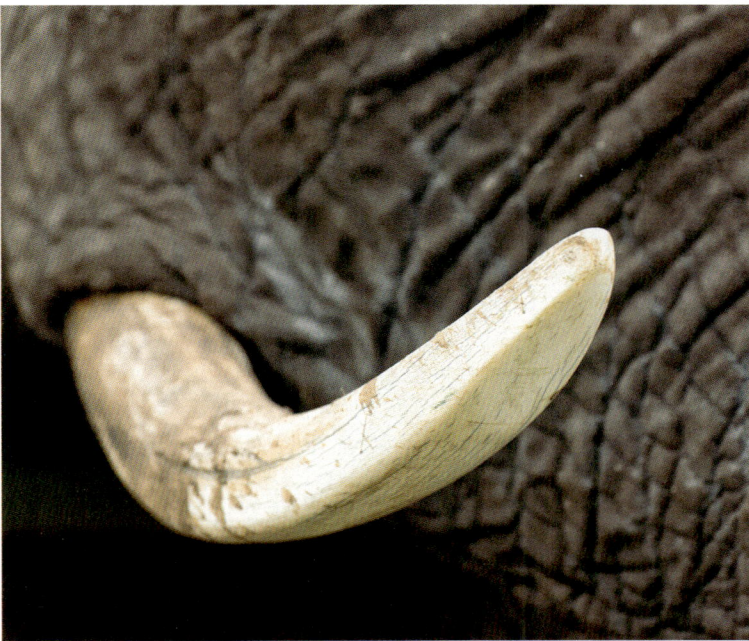

Info George Orwell

Eric Arthur Blair was born in British India on 25 June 1903. He went to school in England before returning to the colony as an imperial policeman in Burma. Being dissatisfied with Britain's colonial rule, he resigned and became a writer, using the pseudonym George Orwell for his literary work. Later, he joined the Spanish Republicans in their struggle against Franco's regime. In his books, Orwell reflects on his personal experience as well as his political views. His work includes colonial literature like his first novel, *Burmese Days,* and the famous works *Animal Farm* and *1984,* in which he anticipated many features of a modern dictatorship. Suffering from tuberculosis, Orwell died on 21 January 1950, three months after his wedding.

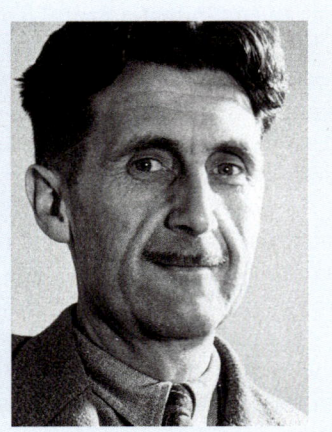

A2 Working for the Empire

Look back at lines 1–130 of the essay 'Shooting and Elephant' and complete tasks 1–6.

Comprehension

1 Complete the sentences below by ticking the correct answer. Only one option is correct.

a Orwell works as a/an …
- ○ **A** referee.
- ○ **B** football player.
- ○ **C** imperial police officer.
- ○ **D** young Buddhist priest in Moulmein, Burma.

b The Burmese …
- ○ **A** help Orwell during a football match.
- ○ **B** work hard to please their British masters.
- ○ **C** start a riot against the British colonial government.
- ○ **D** disrespect and tease Europeans whenever possible.

c In Orwell's view, the British colonial administration …
- ○ **A** is a dictatorship oppressing its population.
- ○ **B** should punish the Burmese for their cheeky behaviour.
- ○ **C** is flawed but still better than most other forms of government.
- ○ **D** contributes to the development of the country and helps people escape poverty.

d One morning, Orwell is called to …
    A buy an elephant.
    B investigate a murder.
    C stop a riot at a local bazaar.
    D stop an elephant which has gone wild.

e The huge animal has already …
    A seriously injured the driver of a rubbish van.
    B killed its mahout and turned over a rubbish van.
    C eaten a cow and destroyed somebody's bamboo hut.
    D destroyed a hut, raided food stalls and destroyed a municipal van.

f When Orwell is almost certain that the whole story has been made up, he …
    A finds the elephant chasing a crowd of naked children.
    B comes across the body of a man killed by the elephant.
    C witnesses how the elephant kills a black Dravidian coolie.
    D sees an old woman attacking a man with a switch in her hand.

g When Orwell eventually finds the elephant on a paddy field, …
    A the animal is still out of control and he shoots it right away.
    B there is a fight between the crowd of Burmese spectators and the police.
    C he decides that the elephant no longer poses a threat and returns home.
    D the elephant appears calm and he feels that it is unnecessary to shoot it.

Analysis

2 Illustrate the elephant's behaviour and Orwell's reaction to it.

3 Look back at ll. 1–40. Examine Orwell's relationship with the local Burmese population.

4 Point out Orwell's perception of Britain's colonial rule in Burma as well as his perception of his job.

Beyond the text

5 `Writing` Imagine you are Orwell, one day before the incident. Write a letter to a friend in which you complain about the way the British dominate the local Burmese population.

6 `Speaking` Work in pairs. Act out a dialogue between Orwell and a man from the Burmese village in which they discuss whether the elephant should be shot.

British forces entering Mandalay, Burma, in 1885. Burma gained independence from the UK in 1948.

A3 The pressure to act

Look back at the second part of Orwell's essay 'Shooting an Elephant'
(lines 131–257) and complete tasks 1–5.

Comprehension

1 Complete the sentences below using information from the text.

A When Orwell decides to go home without shooting the elephant, he looks back and is

surprised to see that _____.

B The villagers urge him to _____.

C In this situation, he understands that, as a European in Burma, he has to _____

_____.

D Orwell does not want to shoot the elephant because _____

_____.

E He fears that the elephant might _____

_____.

F More importantly, he cannot bear the thought that the Burmese _____

_____.

G When Orwell shoots at the elephant, he is shocked that the huge animal _____

_____.

H Even after being hit by multiple bullets, it takes _____

_____ for the elephant to die.

I The local citizens rush towards the animal and _____

_____.

J When the elephant has died, people _____

_____.

Analysis

2 Use the following quote as a starting point to analyse the relationship between the colonizers and the colonized in Orwell's essay.

> 'I perceived in this moment that when the white man turns tyrant it is his own freedom that he destroys.' (ll. 147–148)

3 In groups of 3 to 5 students, discuss the ways in which Orwell criticizes the British Empire in his essay.

Beyond the text

4 YOU CHOOSE:

a Writing Imagine you are Orwell. Write his diary entry one week after shooting the elephant.
OR
b Writing Imagine you are the elephant's owner. Write an interior monologue in which you reflect on the incident, the consequences this has had for you, and whether this has changed how you feel about being a subject of the British Empire.

5 Examine why the elephant has often been interpreted as a metaphor for the British Empire.

A4 Reflecting on colonialism

1 a Describe the cartoon below.

www.CartoonStock.com

"Would you believe that, back home, they're bona fide football supporters who detest all forms of violence ?"

b Explain the message of the cartoon. Assess how it expresses disapproval of Britain's colonial past.

Part B
My Son the Fanatic

B1 My Son the Fanatic *Hanif Kureishi*

'My Son the Fanatic' was written by British author Hanif Kureishi and published in *The New Yorker* in 1994. The short story examines the tensions between a Pakistani immigrant and his son about their cultural identity in England. Read the text and complete the tasks that follow on pp. 30–33.

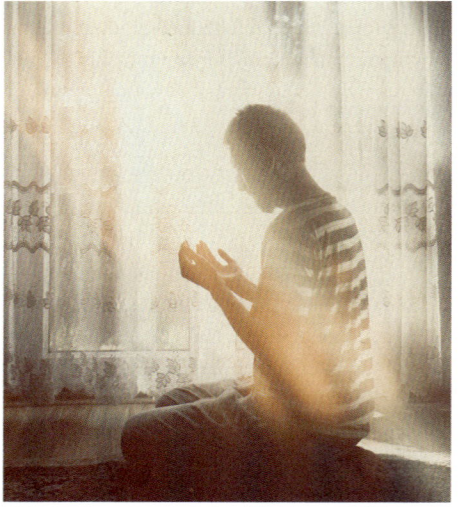

Surreptitiously, the father began going into his son's bedroom. He would sit there for hours, rousing himself only to seek clues. What bewildered him was that Ali was getting tidier. The
5 room, which was usually a tangle of clothes, books, cricket bats and video games, was becoming neat and ordered; spaces began appearing where before there had been only mess.

Initially, Parvez had been pleased: his son was
10 outgrowing his teenage attitudes. But one day, beside the dustbin, Parvez found a torn shopping bag that contained not only old toys but computer discs, videotapes, new books and fashionable clothes the boy had bought a few months before. Also without explanation, Ali had parted from the English girlfriend who
15 used to come around to the house. His old friends stopped ringing.

For reasons he didn't himself understand, Parvez was unable to bring up the subject of Ali's unusual behaviour. He was aware that he had become slightly afraid of his son, who, between his silences, was developing a sharp tongue. One remark Parvez did make – 'You don't
20 play your guitar any more' – elicited the mysterious but conclusive reply, 'There are more important things to be done.'

Yet Parvez felt his son's eccentricity as an injustice. He had always been aware of the pitfalls that other men's sons had stumbled into in England. It was for Ali that Parvez worked long hours; he spent a lot
25 of money paying for Ali's education as an accountant. He had bought Ali good suits, all the books he required, and a computer. And now the boy was throwing his possessions out! The TV, video-player and stereo system followed the guitar. Soon the room was practically bare. Even the unhappy walls bore pale marks where Ali's pictures had been
30 removed.

1 **surreptitious**
[ˌsʌrəpˈtɪʃəs] done in
secret
3 **bewilder sb.** [bɪˈwɪldə]
confuse sb., puzzle sb.
5 **tangle** (n) mess, chaos
20 **elicit sth.** [ɪˈlɪsɪt] *etwas
hervorrufen*
23 **pitfall** trap
25 **accountant**
Buchhalter/in
29 **bear (bore, borne) sth.**
(v) (here) reveal sth.

Parvez couldn't sleep; he went more often to the whisky bottle, even when he was at work. He realised it was imperative to discuss the matter with someone sympathetic.

Parvez had been a taxi-driver for twenty years. Half that time he'd
35 worked for the same firm. Like him, most of the other drivers were Punjabis. They preferred to work at night, when the roads were clearer and the money better. They slept during the day, avoiding their wives. They led almost a boy's life together in the cabbies' office, playing cards and setting up practical jokes, exchanging lewd stories, eating
40 takeaways from local balti houses and discussing politics and their problems.

But Parvez had been unable to discuss the subject of Ali with his friends. He was too ashamed. And he was afraid, too, that they would blame him for the wrong turning his boy had taken, just as he had
45 blamed other fathers whose sons began running around with bad girls, skipping school and joining gangs.

For years, Parvez had boasted to the other men about how Ali excelled in cricket, swimming and football, and what an attentive scholar he was, getting straight As in most subjects. Was it asking too
50 much for Ali to get a good job, marry the right girl and start a family?

Once this happened, Parvez would be happy. His dreams of doing well in England would have come true. Where had he gone wrong?

One night, sitting in the taxi office on busted chairs with his two closest friends, watching a Sylvester Stallone film, Parvez broke his
55 silence.

'I can't understand it!' he burst out. 'Everything is going from his room. And I can't talk to him any more. We were not father and son – we were brothers! Where has he gone? Why is he torturing me?' And Parvez put his head in his hands.
60 Even as he poured out his account, the men shook their heads and gave one another knowing glances.

'Tell me what is happening!' he demanded.

The reply was almost triumphant. They had guessed something was going wrong. Now it was clear: Ali was taking drugs and selling his
65 possessions to pay for them. That was why his bedroom was being emptied.

'What must I do, then?'

Parvez's friends instructed him to watch Ali scrupulously and to be severe with him, before the boy went mad, overdosed or murdered
70 someone.

Parvez staggered out into the early-morning air, terrified that they were right. His boy – the drug-addict killer!

To his relief he found Bettina sitting in his car.

Usually the last customers of the night were local 'brasses', or
75 prostitutes. The taxi-drivers knew them well and often drove them to

32 **imperative** [ɪmˈperətɪv] (adj) urgent and necessary
36 **Punjabi** (n) (here) person originating from Punjab, a region in India and Pakistan
39 **lewd** [luːd, ljuːd] *anstößig*
40 **balti house** restaurant that serves balti, a type of Indian food
53 **busted** (here) broken
60 **pour** [pɔː] **out your account** tell your story
68 **watch sb. scrupulously** observe sb. closely
69 **severe** [sɪˈvɪə] strict

liaisons. At the end of the girls' night, the men would ferry them home, though sometimes they would join the cabbies for a drinking session in the office. Occasionally, the drivers would go with the girls.

'A ride in exchange for a ride,' it was called.

80 Bettina had known Parvez for three years. She lived outside the town and, on the long drives home, during which she sat not in the passenger seat but beside him, Parvez had talked to her about his life and hopes, just as she talked about hers. They saw each other most nights.

85 He could talk to her about things he'd never be able to discuss with his own wife. Bettina, in turn, always reported on her night's activities. He liked to know where she had been and with whom.

Once, he had rescued her from a violent client, and since then they had come to care for each other.

90 Though Bettina had never met Ali, she heard about the boy continually. That night, when Parvez told Bettina that he suspected Ali was on drugs, to Parvez's relief, she judged neither him nor the boy, but said, 'It's all in the eyes.' They might be bloodshot; the pupils might be dilated; Ali might look tired. He could be liable to sweats, or sudden
95 mood changes. 'OK?'

Parvez began his vigil gratefully. Now that he knew what the problem might be, he felt better. And surely, he figured, things couldn't have gone too far?

He watched each mouthful the boy took. He sat beside him at every
100 opportunity and looked into his eyes. When he could, he took the boy's hand, checked his temperature. If the boy wasn't at home, Parvez was active, looking under the carpet, in Ali's drawers and behind the empty wardrobe – sniffing, inspecting, probing. He knew what to look for: Bettina had drawn pictures of capsules, syringes, pills, powders, rocks.

105 Every night, she waited to hear news of what he'd witnessed. After a few days of constant observation, Parvez was able to report that although the boy had given up sports, he seemed healthy. His eyes were clear. He didn't – as Parvez expected he might – flinch guiltily from his father's gaze. In fact, the boy seemed more alert and steady
110 than usual: as well as being sullen, he was very watchful. He returned his father's long looks with more than a hint of criticism, of reproach, even – so much so that Parvez began to feel that it was he who was in the wrong, and not the boy.

'And there's nothing else physically different?' Bettina asked.
115 'No!' Parvez thought for a moment. 'But he is growing a beard.'

One night, after sitting with Bettina in an all-night coffee shop, Parvez came home particularly late. Reluctantly, he and Bettina had abandoned the drug theory, for Parvez had found nothing resembling any drug in Ali's room. Besides, Ali wasn't selling his belongings. He
120 threw them out, gave them away or donated them to charity shops.

[76] **liaison** [li'eɪzn] (here) secret sexual relationship
ferry sb./sth. drive sb./sth. from one place to another
[79] **ride** (n, sl) sexual intercourse
[94] **dilated** (here) wide open
be liable to sth. anfällig sein für etwas
[96] **vigil** ['vɪdʒɪl] Nachtwache
[104] **syringe** [sɪ'rɪndʒ] Spritze
[108] **flinch from sth.** avoid sth. unpleasant (e. g. a look)
[110] **sullen** grumpy, in a bad mood

Standing in the hall, Parvez heard the boy's alarm clock go off.

Parvez hurried into his bedroom, where his wife, still awake, was sewing in bed. He ordered her to sit down and keep quiet, though she had neither stood up nor said a word. As she watched him curiously, he
125　observed his son through the crack of the door.

The boy went into the bathroom to wash. When he returned to his room, Parvez sprang across the hall and set his ear at Ali's door. A muttering sound came from within. Parvez was puzzled but relieved.

Once this clue had been established, Parvez watched him at other
130　times. The boy was praying. Without fail, when he was at home, he prayed five times a day.

Parvez had grown up in Lahore, where all young boys had been taught the Koran. To stop Parvez from falling asleep while he studied, the maulvi had attached a piece of string to the ceiling and tied it to
135　Parvez's hair, so if his head fell forward, he would instantly jerk awake. After this indignity, Parvez had avoided all religions. Not that the other taxi-drivers had any more respect than he. In fact, they made jokes about the local mullahs walking around with their caps and beards, thinking they could tell people how to live, while their eyes roved over
140　the boys and girls in their care.

Parvez described to Bettina what he had discovered. He informed the men in the taxi office. His friends, who had been so inquisitive before, now became oddly silent. They could hardly condemn the boy for his devotions.

145　Parvez decided to take a night off and go out with the boy. They could talk things over. He wanted to hear how things were going at college; he wanted to tell him stories about their family in Pakistan.

More than anything, he yearned to understand how Ali had discovered the 'spiritual dimension', as Bettina called it.

150　To Parvez's surprise, the boy refused to accompany him. He claimed he had an appointment. Parvez had to insist that no appointment could be more important than that of a son with his father.

The next day, Parvez went immediately to the street where Bettina stood in the rain wearing high heels, a short skirt and a long mac,
155　which she would open hopefully at passing cars.

'Get in, get in!' he said.

They drove out across the moors and parked at the spot where, on better days, their view unimpeded for miles except by wild deer and horses, they'd lie back, with their eyes half-closed, saying, 'This is the
160　life.' This time Parvez was trembling. Bettina put her arms around him.

'What's happened?'

'I've just had the worst experience of my life.'

As Bettina rubbed his head, Parvez told her that the previous evening, as he and his son had studied the menu, the waiter, whom
165　Parvez knew, brought him his usual whisky-and-water. Parvez was so

128 **mutter** (v) murmur, speak to yourself
134 **maulvi** ['mɔːlvi] religious teacher of Islam
136 **indignity** humiliation
139 **rove over sb.** look at st. with (sexual) desire
142 **inquisitive** [ɪnˈkwɪzətɪv] nosy, asking a lot of questions
144 **devotion** *Hingabe*
154 **mac** raincoat
158 **unimpeded** [ˌʌn-ɪːˈpiːdɪd] (fml) not blocked by anything

nervous he had even prepared a question. He was going to ask Ali if he was worried about his imminent exams. But first he loosened his tie, crunched a poppadum and took a long drink.

Before Parvez could speak, Ali made a face.

170   'Don't you know it's wrong to drink alcohol?' he had said.

'He spoke to me very harshly,' Parvez said to Bettina. 'I was about to castigate the boy for being insolent, but I managed to control myself.'

Parvez had explained patiently that for years he had worked more than ten hours a day, had few enjoyments or hobbies, and never went

175   on holiday. Surely it wasn't a crime to have a drink when he wanted one?

'But it is forbidden,' the boy said.

Parvez shrugged, 'I know.'

'And so is gambling, isn't it?'

180   'Yes. But surely we are only human?'

Each time Parvez took a drink, the boy winced or made a fastidious face as an accompaniment. This made Parvez drink more quickly. The waiter, wanting to please his friend, brought another glass of whisky. Parvez knew he was getting drunk, but he couldn't stop himself. Ali

185   had a horrible look, full of disgust and censure. It was as if he hated his father.

Halfway through the meal, Parvez suddenly lost his temper and threw a plate on the floor. He felt like ripping the cloth from the table, but the waiters and other customers were staring at him. Yet he

190   wouldn't stand for his own son's telling him the difference between right and wrong. He knew he wasn't a bad man. He had a conscience.

There were a few things of which he was ashamed, but on the whole he had lived a decent life.

[167] **imminent** about to take place
[168] **crunch** (v) *(hier)* *knabbern*
poppadum, poppadom [ˈpɒpədəm] crispy Indian bread
[172] **castigate sb.** scold sb., reprimand sb. (especially a child)
insolent [ˈɪnsələnt] impertinent, rude
[181] **fastidious** [fæˈstɪdiəs] (here) critical
[185] **censure** [ˈsɛnʃə] (n) condemnation

'When have I had time to be wicked?' he asked Ali.

195 In a low monotonous voice the boy explained that Parvez had not, in fact, lived a good life. He had broken countless rules of the Koran.

'For instance?' Parvez demanded.

Ali didn't need to think. As if he had been waiting for this moment, he asked his father if he didn't relish pork pies.

200 'Well.' Parvez couldn't deny that he loved crispy bacon smothered with mushrooms and mustard and sandwiched between slices of fried bread. In fact, he ate this for breakfast every morning.

Ali then reminded Parvez that he had ordered his wife to cook pork sausages, saying to her, 'You're not in the village now. This is England.
205 We have to fit in.'

Parvez was so annoyed and perplexed by this attack that he called for more drink.

'The problem is this,' the boy said. He leaned across the table. For the first time that night his eyes were alive. 'You are too implicated in
210 Western civilisation.'

Parvez burped; he thought he was going to choke. 'Implicated!' he said. 'But we live here!'

'The Western materialists hate us,' Ali said. 'Papa, how can you love something which hates you?'

215 'What is the answer, then,' Parvez said miserably, 'according to you?'

Ali didn't need to think. He addressed his father fluently, as if Parvez were a rowdy crowd which had to be quelled or convinced.

The law of Islam would rule the world; the skin of the infidel would
220 burn off again and again; the Jews and Christers would be routed. The West was a sink of hypocrites, adulterers, homosexuals, drug users and prostitutes.

While Ali talked, Parvez looked out the window as if to check that they were still in England.

225 'My people have taken enough. If the persecution doesn't stop, there will be jihad. I, and millions of others, will gladly give our lives for the cause.'

'But why, why?' Parvez said.

'For us, the reward will be in Paradise.'

230 'Paradise!'

Finally, as Parvez's eyes filled with tears, the boy urged him to mend his ways.

'But how would that be possible?' Parvez asked.

'Pray,' urged Ali. 'Pray beside me.'

235 Parvez paid the bill and ushered his boy out of there as soon as he was able. He couldn't take any more.

Ali sounded as if he'd swallowed someone else's voice.

[194] **wicked** (adj) morally bad
[199] **relish sth.** ['relɪʃ] enjoy sth.
[200] **smother sb./sth.** (here) completely cover sb./sth.
[209] **implicated in sth.** involved in sth., entangled in sth.
[211] **burp** (v) *aufstoßen* **choke** (v) *ersticken*
[218] **quell sth.** suppress sth.
[219] **infidel** ['ɪnfɪdəl, 'ɪnfɪdel] sb. who does not believe in a certain religion
[220] **rout sb.** (v) completely defeat sb., destroy sb.
[221] **hypocrite** ['hɪpəkrɪt] person who pretends to be a morally upright **adulterer** sb. who has sex outside of marriage
[226] **jihad** holy Islamic war
[231] **mend sth.** correct sth.
[235] **usher sb.** guide sb., lead sb.

On the way home, the boy sat in the back of the taxi, as if he were a customer. 'What has made you like this?' Parvez asked him, afraid
240 that somehow he was to blame for all this. 'Is there a particular event which has influenced you?'

'Living in this country.'

'But I love England,' Parvez said, watching his boy in the rear-view mirror. 'They let you do almost anything here.'

245 'That is the problem,' Ali replied.

For the first time in years, Parvez couldn't see straight. He knocked the side of the car against a lorry, ripping off the wing mirror. They were lucky not to have been stopped by the police: Parvez would have lost his licence and his job.

250 Back at the house, as he got out of the car, Parvez stumbled and fell in the road, scraping his hands and ripping his trousers. He managed to haul himself up. The boy didn't even offer him his hand.

Parvez told Bettina he was willing to pray, if that was what the boy wanted – if it would dislodge the pitiless look from his eyes. 'But what
255 I object to,' he said, 'is being told by my own son that I am going to Hell!'

What had finished Parvez off was the boy's saying he was giving up his studies in accounting. When Parvez had asked why, Ali said sarcastically that it was obvious. 'Western education cultivates an
260 anti-religious attitude.' And in the world of accountants it was usual to meet women, drink alcohol and practise usury.

'But it's well-paid work,' Parvez argued. 'For years you've been preparing!'

Ali said he was going to begin to work in prisons, with poor Muslims
265 who were struggling to maintain their purity in the face of corruption.

254 **dislodge sth. from sth.** (here) remove sth. from sth.
261 **usury** [ˈjuːʒəri] *Wucher*
265 **corruption** (here) immorality

Finally, at the end of the evening, as Ali went up to bed, he had asked his father why he didn't have a beard, or at least a moustache.

'I feel as if I've lost my son,' Parvez told Bettina. 'I can't bear to be looked at as if I'm a criminal. I've decided what to do.'

270 'What is it?'

'I'm going to tell him to pick up his prayer mat and get out of my house. It will be the hardest thing I've ever done, but tonight I'm going to do it.'

'But you mustn't give up on him,' said Bettina. 'Many young people 275 fall into cults and superstitious groups. It doesn't mean they'll always feel the same way.' She said Parvez had to stick by his boy.

Parvez was persuaded that she was right, even though he didn't feel like giving his son more love when he had hardly been thanked for all he had already given.

280 For the next two weeks, Parvez tried to endure his son's looks and reproaches. He attempted to make conversation about Ali's beliefs.

But if Parvez ventured any criticism, Ali always had a brusque reply.

On one occasion, Ali accused Parvez of 'grovelling' to the whites; in contrast, he explained, he was not 'inferior'; there was more to the 285 world than the West, though the West always thought it was best.

'How is it you know that?' Parvez said. 'Seeing as you've never left England?'

Ali replied with a look of contempt.

One night, having ensured there was no alcohol on his breath, 290 Parvez sat down at the kitchen table with Ali. He hoped Ali would compliment him on the beard he was growing, but Ali didn't appear to notice it.

The previous day, Parvez had been telling Bettina that he thought people in the West sometimes felt inwardly empty and that people 295 needed a philosophy to live by.

'Yes,' Bettina had said. 'That's the answer. You must tell him what your philosophy of life is. Then he will understand that there are other beliefs.'

After some fatiguing consideration, Parvez was ready to begin. The 300 boy watched him as if he expected nothing.

Haltingly, Parvez said that people had to treat one another with respect, particularly children their parents. This did seem, for a moment, to affect the boy. Heartened, Parvez continued. In his view, this life was all there was, and when you died, you rotted in the earth.

305 'Grass and flowers will grow out of my grave, but something of me will live on.'

'How then?'

'In other people. For instance, I will continue – in you.'

At this the boy appeared a little distressed.

---

275 **superstitious** [ˌsuːpə-ˈstɪʃəs] *abergläubisch*
281 **reproach** (n) accusation
282 **venture sth.** (here) risk to express sth.
283 **grovel** (v) [ˈgrɒvl] behave in a subservient manner
301 **halting** [ˈhɔːltɪŋ] (adj) hesitant
303 **hearten sb.** encourage sb.

310 'And in your grandchildren,' Parvez added for good measure. 'But ³¹⁶**pit** (n) wide hole
while I am here on earth I want to make the best of it. And I want you
to, as well!'

'What d'you mean by "make the best of it"?' asked the boy.

'Well,' said Parvez. 'For a start … you should enjoy yourself. Yes.
315 Enjoy yourself without hurting others.'

Ali said that enjoyment was a 'bottomless pit'.

'But I don't mean enjoyment like that,' said Parvez. 'I mean the
beauty of living.'

'All over the world our people are oppressed,' was the boy's reply.

320 'I know,' Parvez replied, not entirely sure who 'our people' were,
'but still – life is for living!'

Ali said, 'Real morality has existed for hundreds of years. Around
the world millions and millions of people share my beliefs. Are you
saying you are right and they are all wrong?' Ali looked at his father
325 with such aggressive confidence that Parvez would say no more.

A few evenings later, Bettina was riding in Parvez's car after visiting
a client when they passed a boy on the street.

'That's my son,' Parvez said, his face set hard. They were on the
other side of town, in a poor district, where there were two mosques.
330 Bettina turned to see. 'Slow down then, slow down!'

She said, 'He's good-looking. Reminds me of you. But with a more
determined face. Please, can't we stop?'

'What for?'

'I'd like to talk to him.'

335 Parvez turned the cab round and stopped beside the boy.

'Coming home?' Parvez asked. 'It's quite a way.'

The boy shrugged and got into the back seat. Bettina sat in the front. Parvez became aware of Bettina's short skirt, her gaudy rings and ice-blue eyeshadow. He became conscious that the smell of her

340 perfume, which he loved, filled the cab. He opened the window.

While Parvez drove as fast as he could, Bettina said gently to Ali, 'Where have you been?'

'The mosque,' he said.

'And how are you getting on at college? Are you working hard?'

345 'Who are you to ask me these questions?' he said, looking out of the window. Then they hit bad traffic, and the car came to a standstill.

By now, Bettina had inadvertently laid her hand on Parvez's shoulder. She said, 'Your father, who is a good man, is very worried about you. You know he loves you more than his own life.'

350 'You say he loves me,' the boy said.

'Yes!' said Bettina.

'Then why is he letting a woman like you touch him like that?'

If Bettina looked at the boy in anger, he looked back at her with cold fury.

355 She said, 'What kind of woman am I that deserves to be spoken to like that?'

'You know what kind,' he said. Then he turned to his father. 'Now let me out.'

'Never,' Parvez replied.

360 'Don't worry, I'm getting out,' Bettina said.

'No, don't!' said Parvez. But even as the car moved forward, she opened the door and threw herself out – she had done this before – and ran away across the road. Parvez stopped and shouted after her several times, but she had gone.

365 Parvez took Ali back to the house, saying nothing more to him. Ali went straight to his room. Parvez was unable to read the paper, watch television or even sit down. He kept pouring himself drinks.

At last, he went upstairs and paced up and down outside Ali's room. When, finally, he opened the door, Ali was praying. The boy didn't

370 even glance his way.

Parvez kicked him over. Then he dragged the boy up by the front of his shirt and hit him. The boy fell back. Parvez hit him again. The boy's face was bloody. Parvez was panting; he knew that the boy was unreachable, but he struck him none the less. The boy neither covered

375 himself nor retaliated; there was no fear in his eyes. He only said, through his split lip: 'So who's the fanatic now?'

From: Love in a Blue Time*, London: Faber and Faber, 1997*

338 **gaudy** ['gɔːdi] *kitschig*
347 **inadvertent** unintentional
368 **pace** (v) walk
373 **pant** (v) breathe quickly to catch your breath
375 **retaliate** [rɪ'tælieɪt] fight back

Info Hanif Kureishi

Hanif Kureishi (born 5 December 1954, in London) is considered one of Britain's most influential writers. His grandfather had been an affluent colonel in the Indian army before taking his family to Pakistan after the partition
5 of the former British colony of India into the independent states of India and Pakistan in 1947. Later, Kureishi's father emigrated to England where he met Kureishi's English mother, Audrey Buss.
   After receiving his A levels, Kureishi studied philosophy.
10 His works include novels, dramas, short stories and screenplays.

First reaction

1 a Think: What is your first reaction to the short story and its title? Take short notes.
  b Pair: Exchange your ideas with a partner.
  c Share: `Speaking` Present your findings to the class.
2 a Together with a partner, come up with a definition of the term 'fanatic'. You can also use a dictionary or the internet for research.
  b Give at least three suitable examples of fanatic behaviour.

1. _____

2. _____

3. _____

Comprehension

3 Read the short story and put the following sentences in the right
order. Write the numbers 1 to 12 in the column on the right after
each sentence.

Sentence	Number
A After dinner, Ali explains that he is going to quit his education to help Muslims in prison.	
B Ali has stopped playing the guitar.	
C Parvez invites Ali to a restaurant, where Ali expresses his disapproval of his father's habits such as drinking alcohol and eating pork, which are forbidden by the Koran.	
D Ali blames his father for having adopted too much of the liberal Western culture and warns of an impending jihadist backlash.	
E Parvez tries to teach his son that he has to enjoy life while he can. Ali rejects that notion on moral grounds.	
F Parvez, a taxi driver, is too ashamed to bring up the changes in Ali with his friends because he has always been proud of his son's exemplary behaviour.	
G Parvez is worried because his son has suddenly become tidy and has started throwing out all his favourite games and clothes.	
H Ali insults Bettina when she tries to reason with him. Later that evening, Parvez snaps and beats his son, who refuses to fight back.	
I Parvez's friends warn him that Ali has become a drug addict and is selling his belongings to finance his addiction.	
J Parvez discusses his son's strange behaviour with his friend Bettina, who works as a prostitute.	
K Parvez does not discover any clues to sustain the theory that Ali is taking drugs and instead finds him in his room praying five times a day.	
L Parvez works long hours to provide for his son's accounting education and for his comfort at home.	

4 Point out Ali's change of character.
5 Describe Parvez's development from his childhood in Lahore to his
life as an immigrant in England.

Analysis

6 Examine Parvez's relationship with Bettina.

7 Compare Parvez's and Ali's views of living in England as (Muslim) immigrants. Use the following quotes as a starting point:

> Parvez: 'You're not in the village now. This is England. We have to fit in.' (ll. 204–205)

> Ali: 'You are too implicated in Western civilisation.' (ll. 209–210)

> – Parvez: 'They let you do almost anything here.'
> – Ali: 'That is the problem'. (ll. 244–245)

8 Read the scene at the restaurant again (ll. 163–236). Examine the language Parvez and Ali use to try to convince each other.

> **Info Language**
> When analysing language, it is important to be aware of how the text is written. To do so, you need to find certain language features and explain their possible effect. These include the choice of words, the sentence structure (e.g. short / long / simple / sophisticated), stylistic devices (e.g. metaphor / alliteration / repetition of words), exclamatory remarks, punctuation, tone (e.g. ironic / happy / angry / sarcastic) and register (e.g. formal / informal / slang).

5

9 Work with a partner. Discuss whether Parvez is a good father. Use examples from the text to support your view.

Beyond the text

10 a In groups of three, prepare a dialogue between Parvez, his wife and Ali after Parvez has beaten Ali.
b Speaking Perform your scene for the class.

11 Writing Write Parvez's letter of apology to his son.

12 'State multiculturalism has failed and left young Muslims vulnerable to radicalization.' Discuss this quote from former British Prime Minister David Cameron at the Munich Security Conference on 5 February 2011. Refer to the short story 'My Son the Fanatic'.

David Cameron at the Munich Security Conference (5 February 2011)

B2 Diversity in the UK

1 a Work with a partner. Each choose one of the statistics below and present your data to your partner. Discuss possible consequences for Britain's society.

b Prepare a short presentation in which you reveal the consequences discussed. Refer to the statistics.

c Speaking Give your presentation to the class.

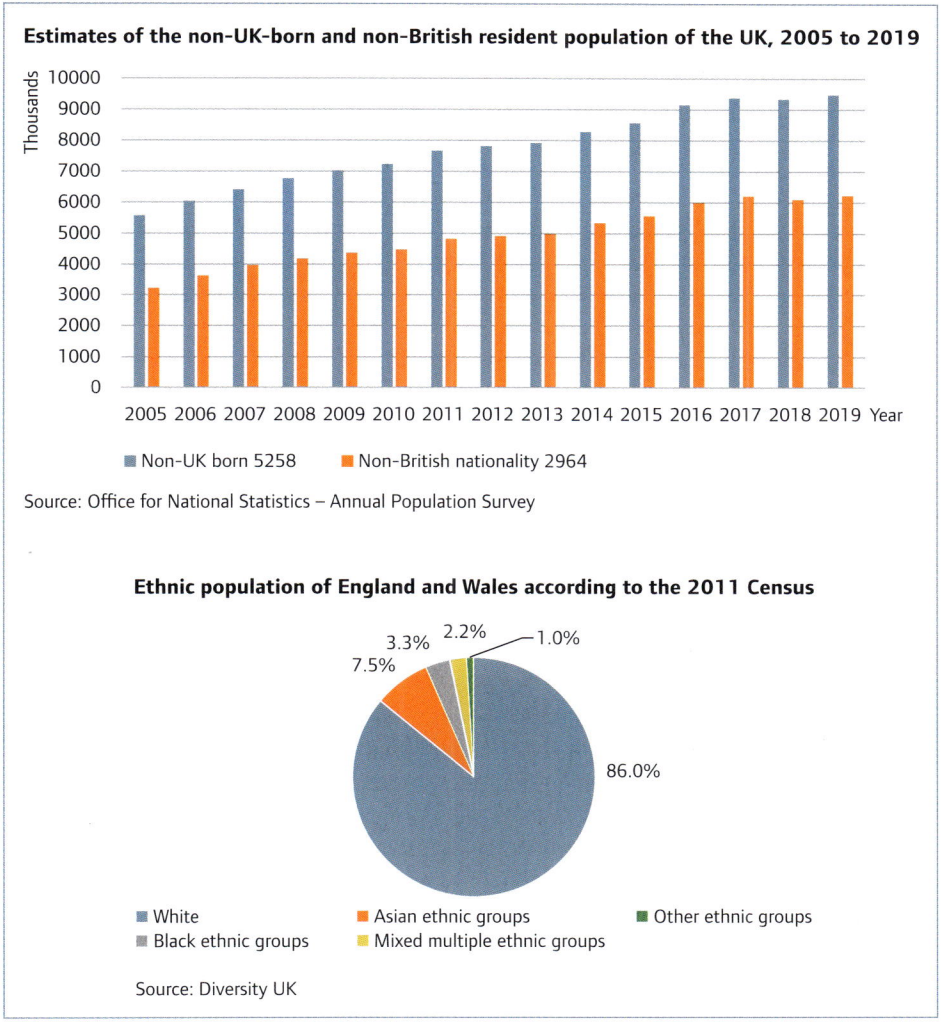

Estimates of the non-UK-born and non-British resident population of the UK, 2005 to 2019

■ Non-UK born 5258 ■ Non-British nationality 2964

Source: Office for National Statistics – Annual Population Survey

Ethnic population of England and Wales according to the 2011 Census

■ White ■ Asian ethnic groups ■ Other ethnic groups
■ Black ethnic groups ■ Mixed multiple ethnic groups

Source: Diversity UK

2 a Read the info box (→ Info box, p. 30) about the author of the short story again.

b Viewing Watch an interview with him provided by the British Library and take notes on his views on culture.

c Speaking Present your findings to your class.

cornelsen.de
Code: webebo

Part C
The Embassy of Cambodia

C1 The Embassy of Cambodia *Zadie Smith*

Zadie Smith first published the short story 'The Embassy of Cambodia' in *The New Yorker* in 2013. The story is set in Willesden, the borough of London where Smith grew up. Read the text and complete the tasks that follow on pp. 52–57.

0–1

Who would expect the Embassy of Cambodia? Nobody. Nobody could have expected it, or be expecting it. It's a surprise, to us all. The
5 Embassy of Cambodia!

Next door to the embassy is a health center. On the other side, a row of private residences, most of them belonging to wealthy Arabs (or so we, the people of Willesden, contend). They have Corinthian pillars on either side of their front doors, and – it's widely believed –
10 swimming pools out back. The embassy, by contrast, is not very grand. It is only a four- or five-bedroom North London suburban villa, built at some point in the thirties, surrounded by a red brick wall, about eight feet high. And back and forth, cresting this wall horizontally, flies a shuttlecock. They are playing badminton in the Embassy of
15 Cambodia. Pock, smash. Pock, smash.

The only real sign that the embassy is an embassy at all is the little brass plaque on the door (which reads, 'THE EMBASSY OF CAMBODIA') and the national flag of Cambodia (we assume that's what it is – what else could it be?) flying from the red tiled roof.
20 Some say, 'Oh, but it has a high wall around it, and this is what signifies that it is not a private residence, like the other houses on the street but, rather, an embassy.' The people who say so are foolish. Many of the private houses have high walls, quite as high as the Embassy of Cambodia's – but they are not embassies.

25 ### 0–2

On the sixth of August, Fatou walked past the embassy for the first time, on her way to a swimming pool. It is a large pool, although not quite Olympic size. To swim a mile you must complete eighty-two lengths, which, in its very tedium, often feels as much a mental exercise
30 as a physical one. The water is kept unusually warm, to please the

²**embassy** [ˈembəsi] official representation of a country in a foreign country
⁶**health center** (AE) private sports centre
⁷**residence** [ˈrezɪdəns] house where people live
⁸**contend sth.** assert sth., claim sth.
⁹**pillar** *Säule*
¹³**eight feet** 2.4 metres
¹⁴**shuttlecock** (BE) = birdie (AE) *Federball*
²⁹**tedium** boredom, monotomy

34

majority of people who patronize the health center, the kind who come not so much to swim as to lounge poolside or rest their bodies in the sauna. Fatou has swum here five or six times now, and she is often the youngest person in the pool by several decades. Generally, the clientele
35 are white, or else South Asian or from the Middle East, but now and then Fatou finds herself in the water with fellow-Africans. When she spots these big men, paddling frantically like babies, struggling simply to stay afloat, she prides herself on her own abilities, having taught herself to swim, several years earlier, at the Carib Beach Resort, in
40 Accra. Not in the hotel pool – no employees were allowed in the pool. No, she learned by struggling through the rough gray sea, on the other side of the resort walls. Rising and sinking, rising and sinking, on the dirty foam. No tourist ever stepped onto the beach (it was covered with trash), much less into the cold and treacherous sea. Nor did any
45 of the other chambermaids. Only some reckless teenage boys, late at night, and Fatou, early in the morning. There is almost no way to compare swimming at Carib Beach and swimming in the health center, warm as it is, tranquil as a bath. And, as Fatou passes the Embassy of Cambodia, on her way to the pool, over the high wall she sees a
50 shuttlecock, passed back and forth between two unseen players. The shuttlecock oats in a wide arc softly rightward, and is smashed back, and this happens again and again, the first player always somehow able to retrieve the smash and transform it, once more, into a gentle, floating arc. High above, the sun tries to force its way through a cloud
55 ceiling, gray and filled with water. Pock, smash. Pock, smash.

0–3

When the Embassy of Cambodia first appeared in our midst, a few years ago, some of us said, 'Well, if we were poets perhaps we could have written some sort of an ode about this surprising appearance of
60 the embassy.' (For embassies are usually to be found in the center of the city. This was the first one we had seen in the suburbs.) But we are not really a poetic people. We are from Willesden. Our minds tend toward the prosaic. I doubt there is a man or woman among us, for example, who – upon passing the Embassy of Cambodia for the first
65 time – did not immediately think: 'genocide.'

0–4

Pock, smash. Pock, smash. This summer we watched the Olympics, becoming well attuned to grunting, and to the many other human sounds associated with effort and the triumph of the will. But the
70 players in the garden of the Embassy of Cambodia are silent. (We can't say for sure that it is a garden – we have a limited view over the wall. It may well be a paved area, reserved for badminton.) The only sign that a game of badminton is under way at all is the motion of the

31 **patronize sb./sth.** [ˈpeɪtrənaɪz] (here) help sb./sth. financially
40 **Accra** [əˈkrɑː, ˈækrə] capital of Ghana
43 **foam** (n) *Schaum*
44 **treacherous** [ˈtretʃərəs] tricky, dangerous
45 **chambermaid** woman who cleans hotel rooms
48 **tranquil** [ˈtræŋkwɪl] (fml) calm
51 **arc** *Bogen*
53 **retrieve sth.** [rɪˈtriːv] (here) catch sth.
65 **genocide** [ˈdʒenəsaɪd] killing of an ethnic group
68 **be attuned to sth.** be familiar with sth.

shuttlecock itself, alternately being lobbed and smashed, lobbed and
75 smashed, and always at the hour that Fatou passes on her way to the
health center to swim (just after ten in the morning on Mondays). It
should be explained that it is Fatou's employers – and not Fatou – who
are the true members of this health club; they have no idea that she
uses their guest passes in this way. (Mr. and Mrs. Derawal and their
80 three children – aged seventeen, fifteen, and ten – live on the same
street as the embassy, but the road is almost a mile long, with the
embassy at one end and the Derawals at the other.) Fatou's deception
is possible only because on Mondays Mr. Derawal drives to Eltham to
visit his mini-market there, and Mrs. Derawal works the counter in
85 the family's second mini-mart, in Kensal Rise. In the slim drawer of a
faux-Louis XVI console, in the entrance hall of the Derawals' primary
residence, one can find a stockpile of guest passes. Nobody besides
Fatou seems to remember that they are there.

 Since August 6th (the first occasion on which she noticed the
90 badminton), Fatou has made a point of pausing by the bus stop
opposite the embassy for five or ten minutes before she goes in to
swim, idle minutes she can hardly afford (Mrs. Derawal returns to
the house at lunchtime) and yet seems unable to forgo. Such is the
strangely compelling aura of the embassy. Usually, Fatou gains nothing
95 from this waiting and observing, but on a few occasions she has seen
people arrive at the embassy and watched as they are buzzed through
the gate. Young white people carrying rucksacks. Often they are
scruffy, and wearing sandals, despite the cool weather. None of the
visitors so far have been visibly Cambodian. These young people are
100 likely looking for visas. They are buzzed in and then pass through the
gate, although Fatou would really have to stand on top of the bus stop
to get a view of whoever it is that lets them in. What she can say with
certainty is that these occasional arrivals have absolutely no effect on
the badminton, which continues in its steady pattern, first gentle, then
105 fast, first soft and high, then hard and low.

0–5

On the twentieth of August, long after the Olympians had returned to
their respective countries, Fatou noticed that a basketball hoop had
appeared in the far corner of the garden, its net of synthetic white
110 rope rising high enough to be seen over the wall. But no basketball
was ever played – at least not when Fatou was passing. The following
week it had been moved closer to Fatou's side of the wall. (It must be a
mobile hoop, on casters.) Fatou waited a week, two weeks, but still no
basketball game replaced the badminton, which carried on as before.

[82] **deception** *Täuschung*
[86] **faux** [fəʊ]-**Louis XVI
console** small table
fixed to the wall that
imitates the style of the
18th century
[92] **idle** [ˈaɪdl] (adj) not
being used
[93] **forgo sth.** (forwent –
forgone) do without
sth.
[94] **compelling** [kəmˈpelɪŋ]
captivating, fascinating
[96] **buzz sth. (for sb./
sth.)** (v, infml) (here)
activate the electronic
buzzer that opens a
door to let sb./sth. in
[113] **caster** small wheel

0–6

115 When I say that we were surprised by the appearance of the Embassy
of Cambodia, I don't mean to suggest that the embassy is in any way
unique in its peculiarity. In fact, this long, wide street is notable for
a number of curious buildings, in the context of which the Embassy
120 of Cambodia does not seem especially strange. There is a mansion
called GARYLAND, with something else in Arabic engraved below
GARYLAND, and both the English and the Arabic text are inlaid in
pink-and-green marble pillars that bookend a gigantic fence, far
higher than the embassy's, better suited to a fortress. Dramatic golden
125 gates open automatically to let vehicles in and out. At any one time,
GARYLAND has five to seven cars parked in its driveway.

There is a house with a huge pink elephant on the doorstep, apparently made of mosaic tiles.

There is a Catholic nunnery with a single red Ford Focus parked in
130 front. There is a Sikh institute. There is a faux-Tudor house with a pool
that Mickey Rooney rented for a season, while he was performing in
the West End fifteen summers ago. That house sits opposite a dingy
retirement home, where one sometimes sees distressed souls, barely
covered by their dressing gowns, standing on their tiny balconies,
135 staring into the tops of the chestnut trees.

So we are hardly strangers to curious buildings, here in Willesden
& Brondesbury. And yet still we find the Embassy of Cambodia a little
surprising. It is not the right sort of surprise, somehow.

0–7

140 In a discarded *Metro* found on the floor of the Derawal kitchen, Fatou
read with interest a story about a Sudanese 'slave' living in a rich man's
house in London. It was not the first time that Fatou had wondered
if she herself was a slave, but this story, brief as it was, confirmed in
her own mind that she was not. After all, it was her father, and not a
145 kidnapper, who had taken her from Ivory Coast to Ghana, and when
they reached Accra they had both found employment in the same
hotel. Two years later, when she was eighteen, it was her father again
who had organized her difficult passage to Libya and then on to Italy –
a not insignificant financial sacrifice on his part. Also, Fatou could read
150 English – and speak a little Italian – and this girl in the paper could not
read or speak anything except the language of her tribe. And nobody
beat Fatou, although Mrs. Derawal had twice slapped her in the face,
and the two older children spoke to her with no respect at all and
thanked her for nothing. (Sometimes she heard her name used as a
155 term of abuse between them. 'You're as black as Fatou.' Or 'You're as
stupid as Fatou.') On the other hand, just like the girl in the newspaper,
she had not seen her passport with her own eyes since she arrived at
the Derawals', and she had been told from the start that her wages

[118] **peculiarity**
[pɪˌkjuːliˈær-əti]
Eigenheit, Besonderheit
[120] **mansion**
[ˈmænʃn] large house
[124] **fortress** *Festung*
[129] **nunnery** *Nonnenkloster*
[130] **faux Tudor house**
[fəʊ ˈtjuːdə] house that
imitates the style of
the 16th century
[132] **dingy** [ˈdɪndʒi]
schmuddelig
[140] **discard sth.** throw sth.
away
Metro [ˈmetrəʊ] UK
newspaper
[155] **abuse** [əˈbjuːs] (n)
insult

were to be retained by the Derawals to pay for the food and water and
160 heat she would require during her stay, as well as to cover the rent for
the room she slept in. In the final analysis, however, Fatou was not
confined to the house. She had an Oyster Card, given to her by the
Derawals, and was trusted to do the food shopping and other outside
tasks for which she was given cash and told to return with change and
165 receipts for everything. If she did not go out in the evenings that was
only because she had no money with which to go out, and anyway
knew very few people in London. Whereas the girl in the paper was
not allowed to leave her employers' premises, not ever – she was a
prisoner.
170   On Sunday mornings, for example, Fatou regularly left the house
to meet her church friend Andrew Okonkwo at the 98 bus stop and go
with him to worship at the Sacred Heart of Jesus, just off the Kilburn
High Road. Afterward Andrew always took her to a Tunisian café,
where they had coffee and cake, which Andrew, who worked as a night
175 guard in the City, always paid for. And on Mondays Fatou swam. In
very warm water, and thankful for the semi-darkness in which the
health club, for some reason, kept its clientele, as if the place were a
night club, or a midnight Mass. The darkness helped disguise the fact
that her swimming costume was in fact a sturdy black bra and a pair
180 of plain black cotton knickers. No, on balance she did not think she
was a slave.

0–8

The woman exiting the Embassy of Cambodia did not look especially
like a New Person or an Old Person – neither clearly of the city nor of
185 the country – and of course it is a long time since this division meant
anything in Cambodia. Nor did these terms mean anything to Fatou,
who was curious only to catch her first sighting of a possible Cambodian
anywhere near the Embassy of Cambodia. She was particularly inter-
ested in the woman's clothes, which were precise and utilitarian – a
190 gray shirt tucked tightly into a pair of tan slacks, a blue mackintosh, a
droopy rain hat – just as if she were a man, or no different from a man.
   Her straight black hair was cut short. She had in her hands many
bags from Sainsbury's, and this Fatou found a little mysterious: where
was she taking all that shopping? It also surprised her that the woman
195 from the Embassy of Cambodia should shop in the same Willesden
branch of Sainsbury's where Fatou shopped for the Derawals. She had
an idea that Oriental people had their own, secret establishments. (She
believed the Jews did, too.) She both admired and slightly resented
this self-reliance, but had no doubt that it was the secret to holding
200 great power, as a people. For example, when the Chinese had come
to Fatou's village to take over the mine, an abiding local mystery had
been: what did they eat and where did they eat it? They certainly did

[162] **Oyster Card** card that
is used to access public
transport in London
[168] **premises** ['premisiz]
(pl) area made up of a
building and the land
on which it stands
[177] **clientele** [ˌkliːənˈtel]
group of customers
[179] **sturdy** robust
[180] **knickers** (pl, BE) =
panties (pl, AE)
women's underwear
[187] **sighting** act of seeing
sth. (esp. sth. rare)
[190] **tan** (adj) (here) light
brown
slacks trousers for
informal wear
mackintosh raincoat
[201] **abiding** (adj, fml)
long-lasting

not buy food in the market, or from the Lebanese traders along the main road. They made their own arrangements. (Whether back home
205 or here, the key to surviving as a people, in Fatou's opinion, was to make your own arrangements.)

But, looking again at the bags the Cambodian woman carried, Fatou wondered whether they weren't in fact very old bags – hadn't their design changed? The more she looked at them the more convinced she
210 became that they contained not food but clothes or something else again, the outline of each bag being a little too rounded and smooth. Maybe she was simply taking out the rubbish. Fatou stood at the bus stop and watched until the Cambodian woman reached the corner, crossed, and turned left toward the high road. Meanwhile, back at
215 the embassy the badminton continued to be played, though with a little more effort now because of a wayward wind. At one point it seemed to Fatou that the next lob would blow southward, sending the shuttlecock over the wall to land lightly in her own hands. Instead the other player, with his vicious reliability (Fatou had long ago decided
220 that both players were men), caught the shuttlecock as it began to drift and sent it back to his opponent – another deathly, downward smash.

0–9

No doubt there are those who will be critical of the narrow, essentially local scope of Fatou's interest in the Cambodian woman from the
225 Embassy of Cambodia, but we, the people of Willesden, have some sympathy with her attitude. The fact is if we followed the history of every little country in this world – in its dramatic as well as its quiet times – we would have no space left in which to live our own lives or to apply ourselves to our necessary tasks, never mind indulge in
230 occasional pleasures, like swimming. Surely there is something to be said for drawing a circle around our attention and remaining within that circle. But how large should this circle be?

0–10

It was the Sunday after Fatou saw the Cambodian that she decided to
235 put a version of this question to Andrew, as they sat in the Tunisian café eating two large fingers of dough stuffed with cream and custard and topped with a strip of chocolate icing. Specifically, she began a conversation with Andrew about the Holocaust, as Andrew was the only person she had found in London with whom she could have these
240 deep conversations, partly because he was patient and sympathetic to her, but also because he was an educated person, currently studying for a part-time business degree at the College of North West London. With his student card he had been given free, twenty-four-hour access to the Internet.

204 **main road** (old-fashioned) high road
216 **wayward** ['weɪwəd] unpredictable, (here) constantly changing
224 **scope** *Umfang*
229 **indulge in sth.** [ɪnˈdʌldʒ] allow yourself to do sth. enjoyable

245 'But more people died in Rwanda,' Fatou argued. 'And nobody speaks about that! Nobody!'

'Yes, I think that's true,' Andrew conceded, and put the first of four sugars in his coffee. 'I have to check. But, yes, millions and millions. They hide the true numbers, but you can see them online. There's
250 always a lot of hiding; it's the same all over. It's like this bureaucratic Nigerian government – they are the greatest at numerology, hiding figures, changing them to suit their purposes. I have a name for it: I call it "demonology." Not "numerology" – "demonology."'

'Yes, but what I am saying is like this,' Fatou pressed, wary of the
255 conversation's drifting back, as it usually did, to the financial corruption of the Nigerian government. 'Are we born to suffer? Sometimes I think we were born to suffer more than all the rest.'

Andrew pushed his professorial glasses up his nose. 'But, Fatou, you're forgetting the most important thing. Who cried most for Jesus?
260 His mother. Who cries most for you? Your father. It's very logical, when you break it down. The Jews cry for the Jews. The Russians cry for the Russians. We cry for Africa, because we are Africans, and, even then, I'm sorry, Fatou' – Andrew's chubby face creased up in a smile – 'if Nigeria plays Ivory Coast and we beat you into the ground, I'm
265 laughing, man! I can't lie. I'm celebrating. Stomp! Stomp!' He did a little dance with his upper body, and Fatou tried, not for the first time, to imagine what he might be like as a husband, but could see only herself as the wife, and Andrew as a teenage son of hers, bright and helpful, to be sure, but a son all the same – though in reality he was three years
270 older than she. Surely it was wrong to find his baby fat and struggling mustache so off-putting. Here was a good man! She knew that he cared for her, was clean, and had given his life to Christ. Still, some part of her rebelled against him, some unholy part.

'Hush your mouth,' she said, trying to sound more playful than
275 disgusted, and was relieved when he stopped jiggling and laid both his hands on the table, his face suddenly quite solemn.

'Believe me, that's a natural law, Fatou, pure and simple. Only God cries for us all, because we are *all* his children. It's very, very logical. You just have to think about it for a moment.'

280 Fatou sighed, and spooned some coffee foam into her mouth. 'But I still think we have more pain. I've seen it myself. Chinese people have never been slaves. They are always protected from the worst.'

Andrew took off his glasses and rubbed them on the end of his shirt. Fatou could tell that he was preparing to lay knowledge upon her.

285 'Fatou, think about it for a moment, please: what about Hiroshima?'

It was a name Fatou had heard before, but sometimes Andrew's superior knowledge made her nervous. She would find herself struggling to remember even the things she had believed she already knew.

253 **demonology** [ˌdiːməˈnɒlədʒi] study of evil spirits
254 **be wary** [ˈweəri] **of sth./sb.** (here) act cautiously because you think sth./sb. might cause problems
275 **jiggle** (v) shake
276 **solemn** [ˈsɒləm] serious

'The big wave …' she began, uncertainly – it was the wrong answer.
290 He laughed mightily and shook his head at her.

'No, man! Big bomb. Biggest bomb in the world, made by the U.S.A., of course. They killed five million people in *one second*. Can you imagine that? You think just because your eyes are like this' – he tugged the skin at both temples – 'you're always protected? Think
295 again. This bomb, even if it didn't blow you up, a week later it melted the skin off your bones.'

Fatou realized that she had heard this story before, or some version of it. But she felt the same vague impatience with it as she did with all accounts of suffering in the distant past. For what could be done about
300 the suffering of the past?

'O.K.,' she said. 'Maybe all people have their hard times, in the past of history, but I still say –'

'Here is a counterpoint,' Andrew said, reaching out and gripping her shoulder. 'Let me ask you, Fatou, seriously, think about this. I'm sorry
305 to interrupt you, but I have thought a lot about this and I want to pass it on to you, because I know you care about things seriously, not like these people.' He waved a hand at the assortment of cake eaters at other tables. 'You're not like the other girls I know, just thinking about the club and their hair. You're a person who thinks. I told you before,
310 anything you want to know about, ask me – I'll look it up, I'll do the research. I have access. Then I'll bring it to you.'

'You're a very good friend to me, Andrew, I know that.'

'Listen, we are friends to each other. In this world you need friends. But, Fatou, listen to my question. It's a counterpoint to what you
315 have been saying. Tell me, why would God choose us especially for suffering when we, above all others, praise his name? Africa is the fastest-growing Christian continent! Just think about it for a minute! It doesn't even make sense!'

'But it's not him,' Fatou said quietly, looking over Andrew's shoulder
320 at the rain beating on the window. 'It's the Devil.'

0–11

Andrew and Fatou sat in the Tunisian coffee shop, waiting for it to stop raining, but it did not stop raining, and at 3 p.m. Fatou said she would just have to get wet. She shared Andrew's umbrella as far as the
325 Overground, letting him pull her into his clammy, high-smelling body as they walked. At Brondesbury station Andrew had to get the train, and so they said goodbye. Several times he tried to press his umbrella on her, but Fatou knew the walk from Acton Central to Andrew's bed-sit was long and she refused to let him suffer on her account.
330 'Big woman. Won't let anybody protect you.'

'Rain doesn't scare me.'

[298] **impatience** [ɪmˈpeɪʃns] *Ungeduld*

[303] **counterpoint** argument against sth.

[325] **Overground** train line above the ground

[329] **on account of sb./ sth.** because of sb./ sth.

Fatou took from her pocket a swimming cap she had found on the floor of the health-club changing room. She wound her plaits into a bun and pulled the cap over her head.

335 'That's a very original idea,' Andrew said, laughing. 'You should market that! Make your first million!'

'Peace be with you,' Fatou said, and kissed him chastely on the cheek. Andrew did the same, lingering a little longer with his kiss than was necessary.

340 **0–12**

By the time Fatou reached the Derawals', only her hair was dry, but before going to get changed she rushed to the kitchen to take the lamb out of the freezer, though it was pointless – there were not enough hours before dinner – and then upstairs to collect the dirty clothes
345 from the matching wicker baskets in four different bedrooms. There was no one in the master bedroom, or in Faizul's, or Julie's. Downstairs a television was blaring. Entering Asma's room, hearing nothing, assuming it empty, Fatou headed straight for the laundry bin in the corner. As she opened the lid she felt a hand hit her hard on the back;
350 she turned around.

There was the youngest, Asma, in front of her, her mouth open like a trout fish. Before Fatou could understand, Asma punched the huge pile of clothes out of her hands. Fatou stooped to retrieve them. While she was kneeling on the floor, another strike came, a kick to
355 her arm. She left the clothes where they were and got up, frightened by her own anger. But when she looked at Asma now she saw the girl gesturing frantically at her own throat, then putting her hands together in prayer, and then back to her throat once more. Her eyes were bulging. She veered suddenly to the right; she threw herself over
360 the back of a chair. When she turned back to Fatou her face was gray and Fatou understood finally and ran to her, grabbed her round her waist, and pulled upward as she had been taught in the hotel. A marble – with an iridescent ribbon of blue at its center, like a wave – flew from the child's mouth and landed wetly in the carpet's plush.

365 Asma wept and drew in frantic gulps of air. Fatou gave her a hug, and worried when the clothes would get done. Together they went down to the den, where the rest of the family was watching 'Britain's Got Talent' on a flat-screen TV attached to the wall.

Everybody stood at the sight of Asma's wild weeping. Mr. Derawal
370 paused the Sky box. Fatou explained about the marble.

'How many times I tell you not to put things in your mouth?' Mr. Derawal asked, and Mrs. Derawal said something in their language – Fatou heard the name of their God – and pulled Asma onto the sofa and stroked her daughter's silky black hair.

333 **wind** [waɪnd] **sb.'s plaits** [plæts] **into a bun** (wound [waʊnd] – wound) (BE) *jds. Zöpfe in einem Dutt zusammenbinden*
337 **chaste** (fml) *keusch*
345 **wicker basket** *Weidenkorb*
353 **retrieve sth.** [rɪˈtriːv] get sth. back
357 **frantically** uncontrollably
359 **bulge** [bʌldʒ] *heraustreten*
362 **marble** *Murmel*
363 **iridescent** [ˌɪrɪˈdesnt] (fml) bright and colourful
367 **den** room of a house where people relax, watch TV, etc.

Marbles

42

375 'I couldn't breathe, man! I couldn't call nobody,' Asma cried. 'I was gonna die!'

'What you putting marbles in your mouth for anyway, you idiot,' Faizul said, and un-paused the Sky box. 'What kind of chief puts a marble in her mouth? Idiot. Bet you was bricking it.'

380 'Oi, she saved your life,' said Julie, the eldest child, whom Fatou generally liked the least. 'Fatou saved your life. That's deep.'

'I woulda just done this,' Faizul said, and performed an especially dramatic Heimlich to his own skinny body. 'And if that didn't work I woulda just start pounding myself karate style, bam bam bam bam
385 bam –'

'Faizul!' Mr. Derawal shouted, and then turned stiffly to Fatou, and spoke not to her, exactly, but to a point somewhere between her elbow and the sunburst mirror behind her head. 'Thank you, Fatou. It's lucky you were there.'

390 Fatou nodded and moved to leave, but at the doorway to the den Mrs. Derawal asked her if the lamb had defrosted and Fatou had to confess that she had only just taken it out. Mrs. Derawal said something sharply in her language. Fatou waited for something further, but Mr. Derawal only smiled awkwardly at her, and nodded as a sign that she
395 could go now. Fatou went upstairs to collect the clothes.

0–13

'To keep you is no benefit. To destroy you is no loss' was one of the mottoes of the Khmer Rouge. It referred to the New People, those city dwellers who could not be made to give up city life and work on a
400 farm. By returning everybody to the land, the regime hoped to create a society of Old People – that is to say, of agrarian peasants. When a New Person was relocated from the city to the country, it was vital not to show weakness in the fields. Vulnerability was punishable by death.

In Willesden, we are almost all New People, though some of us,
405 like Fatou, were, until quite recently, Old People, working the land in our various countries of origin. Of the Old and New People of Willesden I speak; I have been chosen to speak for them, though they did not choose me and must wonder what gives me the right. I could say, 'Because I was born at the crossroads of Willesden, Kilburn, and
410 Queen's Park!' But the reply would be swift and damning: 'Oh, don't be foolish, many people were born right there; it doesn't mean anything at all. We are not one people and no one can speak for us. It's all a lot of nonsense. We see you standing on the balcony, overlooking the Embassy of Cambodia, in your dressing gown, staring into the chestnut
415 trees, looking gormless. The real reason you speak in this way is because you can't think of anything better to do.'

378 **chief** (sl, BE) (here) idiot
379 **you was bricking it** (sl, BE) you were very scared
383 **Heimlich = Heimlich manoeuvre** [ˈhaɪmlɪk mənuːvə] *Heimlich-Manöver zur Rettung erstickender Personen*
399 **city dweller** person who lives in the city
415 **gormless** silly, stupid

0–14

On Monday, Fatou went swimming. She paused to watch the badminton.
She thought that the arm that delivered the smashes must make a
420 movement similar to the one she made in the pool, with her clumsy
yet effective front crawl. She entered the health center and gave a
guest pass to the girl behind the desk. In the dimly lit changing room,
she put on her sturdy black underwear. As she swam, she thought of
Carib Beach. Her father serving snapper to the guests on the deck, his
425 bow tie always a little askew, the ugly tourists, the whole scene there.
Of course, it was not surprising in the least to see old white men from
Germany with beautiful local girls on their laps, but she would never
forget the two old white women from England – red women, really,
thanks to the sun – each of them as big as two women put together,
430 with Kweku and Osai lying by their sides, the boys hooking their
scrawny black bird-arms round the women's massive red shoulders,
dancing with them in the hotel 'ballroom,' answering to the names
Michael and David, and disappearing into the women's cabins at night.
She had known the boys' real girlfriends; they were chambermaids
435 like Fatou. Sometimes they cleaned the rooms where Kweku and Osai
spent the night with the English women. And the girls themselves had
'boyfriends' among the guests. It was not a holy place, that hotel. And
the pool was shaped like a kidney bean: nobody could really swim in
it, or showed any sign of wanting to. Mostly, they stood in it and drank
440 cocktails. Sometimes they even had their burgers delivered to the pool.
Fatou hated to watch her father crouching to hand a burger to a man
waist high in water.

The only good thing that happened in Carib Beach was this: once
a month, on a Sunday, the congregation of a local church poured out
445 of a coach at the front gates, lined up fully dressed in the courtyard,
and then walked into the pool for a mass baptism. The tourists were
never warned, and Fatou never understood why the congregants were
allowed to do it. But she loved to watch their white shirts bloat and
spread across the surface of the water, and to hear the weeping and
450 singing. At the time – though she was not then a member of that
church, or of any church except the one in her heart – she had felt
that this baptism was for her, too, and that it kept her safe, and that
this was somehow the reason she did not become one of the 'girls' at
the Carib Beach Resort. For almost two years – between her father's
455 efforts and the grace of an unseen and unacknowledged God – she did
her work, and swam Sunday mornings at the crack of dawn, and got
along all right. But the Devil was waiting.

She had only a month left in Accra when she entered a bedroom
to clean it one morning and heard the door shut softly behind her
460 before she could put a hand to it. He came, this time, in Russian form.
Afterward, he cried and begged her not to tell anyone: his wife had

[424] **snapper** type of fish
[425] **askew** [əˈskjuː] not quite straight
[427] **lap** *Schoß*
[441] **crouch** [kraʊtʃ] (v) *in die Hocke gehen*
[444] **congregation** *Gemeinde*
[446] **baptism** [ˈbæptɪzəm] *Taufe*

gone to see the Cape Coast Castle and they were leaving the following morning. Fatou listened to his blubbering and realized that he thought the hotel would punish him for his action, or that the police would be
465 called. That was when she knew that the Devil was stupid as well as evil. She spat in his face and left. Thinking about the Devil now made her swimming fast and angry, and for a while she easily lapped the young white man in the lane next to hers, the faster lane.

0–15

470 'Don't give the Devil your anger, it is his food,' Andrew had said to her, when they first met, a year ago. He handed her a leaflet as she sat eating a sandwich on a bench in Kilburn Park. 'Don't make it so easy for him.' Without being invited, he took the seat next to hers and began going through the text of his leaflet. It was printed to look like a
475 newspaper, and he started with the headline: 'WHY IS THERE PAIN?' She liked him. They began a theological conversation. It continued in the Tunisian café, and every Sunday for several months. A lot of the things he said she had heard before from other people, and they did not succeed in changing her attitude. In the end, it was one thing that
480 he said to her that really made the difference. It was after she'd told him this story:

'One day, at the hotel, I heard a commotion on the beach. It was early morning. I went out and I saw nine children washed up dead on the beach. Ten or eleven years old, boys and girls. They had gone
485 into the water, but they didn't know how to swim. Some people were crying, maybe two people. Everyone else just shook their heads and carried on walking to where they were going. After a long time, the police came. The bodies were taken away. People said, "Well, they are with God now." Everybody carried on like before. I went back to
490 work. The next year I arrived in Rome. I saw a boy who was about fifteen years old knocked down on his bike. He was dead. People were screaming and crying in the street. Everybody crying. They were not his family. They were only strangers. The next day, it was in the paper.'

And Andrew replied, 'A tap runs fast the first time you switch it on.'

495 ## 0–16

Twenty more laps. Fatou tried to think of the last time she had cried. It was in Rome, but it wasn't for the boy on the bike. She was cleaning toilets in a Catholic girls' school. She did not know Jesus then, so it made no difference what kind of school it was – she knew only that
500 she was cleaning toilets. At midday, she had a fifteen-minute break. She would go to the little walled garden across the road to smoke a cigarette. One day, she was sitting on a bench near a fountain, and spotted something odd in the bushes. A tin of green paint. A gold spray can. A Statue of Liberty costume. An identity card with the name Rajib

[467] **lap sb.** *jdn. überrunden*
[468] **lane** (here) *Bahn*
[471] **leaflet** *Flugblatt, Handzettel*
[482] **commotion** *agitation, uproar*
[494] **tap** *Wasserhahn*

505 Devanga. One shoe. An empty wallet. A plastic tub with a slit cut in
the top meant for coins and euro notes – empty. A little stain of what
looked like blood on this tub. Until that point, she had been envious of
the Bengali boys on Via Nazionale. She felt that she, too, could paint
herself green and stand still for an hour. But when she tried to find
510 out more the Bengalis would not talk to her. It was a closed shop, for
brown men only. Her place was in the bathroom stalls. She thought
those men had it easy. Then she saw that little sad pile of belongings in
the bush and cried; for herself or for Rajib, she wasn't sure.

Now she turned onto her back in the water for the final two laps,
515 relaxed her arms, and kicked her feet out like a frog. Water made her
think of more water. 'When you're baptized in our church, all sin is
wiped, you start again': Andrew's promise. She had never told Andrew
of the sin precisely, but she knew that he knew she was not a virgin.
The day she finally became a Catholic, February 6, 2011, Andrew had
520 taken her, hair still wet, to the Tunisian café and asked her how it felt.

She was joyful! She said, 'I feel like a new person!'

But happiness like that is hard to hold on to. Back at work the
next day, picking Julie's dirty underwear up off the floor inches from
the wicker basket, she had to keep reminding herself of her new
525 relationship with Jesus and how it changed everything. Didn't it
change everything? The following Sunday she expressed some of her
doubt, cautiously, to Andrew.

'But did you think you'd never feel sad again? Never angry or tired
or just pissed off – sorry about my language. Come on, Fatou! Wise
530 up, man!'

Was it wrong to hope to be happy?

0 – 17

Lost to these watery thoughts, Fatou got home a little later than usual
and was through the door only minutes before Mrs. Derawal.

535 'How is Asma?' Fatou asked. She had heard the girl cry out in the
night.

'My goodness, it was just a little marble,' Mrs. Derawal said, and
Fatou realized that it was not in her imagination: since Sunday night,
neither of the adult Derawals had been able to look her in the eye.
540 'What a fuss everybody is making. I have a list for you – it's on the
table.'

0 – 18

Fatou watched Andrew pick his way through the tables in the Tunisian
café, holding a tray with a pair of mochas on it and some croissants.
545 He hit the elbow of one man with his backside and then trailed the belt
of his long, silly leather coat through the lunch of another, apologizing
as he went. You could not say that he was an elegant man. But he

505 **slit** *Schlitz*
523 **inch** *2,54 cm*
545 **trail sth./sb.** *etwas/
jdn. hinter sich her-
ziehen*

was generous, he was thoughtful. She stood up to push a teetering
croissant back onto its plate. They sat down at the same time, and
550 smiled at each other.

'Awhile ago you asked me about Cambodia,' Andrew said. 'Well, it's
a very interesting case.' He tapped the frame of his glasses. 'If you even
wore a pair of these? They would kill you. Glasses meant you thought
too much. They had very primitive ideas. They were enemies of logic
555 and progress. They wanted everybody to go back to the country and
live like simple people.'

'But sometimes it's true that things are simpler in the country.'

'In some ways. I don't really know. I've never lived in the country.'

I don't really know. It was good to hear him say that! It was a good
560 sign. She smiled cheekily at him. 'People are less sinful in the country,'
she said, but he did not seem to see that she was flirting with him, and
embarked on another lecture:

'That's true. But you can't force people to live in the country. That's
what I call a Big Man Policy. I invented this phrase for my dissertation.
565 We know all about Big Man Policies in Nigeria. They come from the
top, and they crush you. There's always somebody who wants to be
the Big Man, and take everything for himself, and tell everybody how
to think and what to do. When, actually, it's he who is weak. But if the
Big Men see that *you* see that *they* are weak they have no choice but
570 to destroy you. That is the real tragedy.'

Fatou sighed. 'I never met a man who didn't want to tell everybody
how to think and what to do,' she said.

Andrew laughed. 'Fatou, you include me? Are you a feminist now,
too?'

575 Fatou brought her mug up to her lips and looked penetratingly at
Andrew. There were good and bad kinds of weakness in men, and she
had come to the conclusion that the key was to know which kind you
were dealing with.

'Andrew,' she said, putting her hand on his, 'would you like to come
580 swimming with me?'

0–19

Because Fatou believed that the Derawals' neighbors had been
instructed to spy on her, she would not let Andrew come to the house
to pick her up on Monday, instead leaving as she always did, just
585 before ten, carrying misleading Sainsbury's bags and walking toward
the health center. She spotted him from a long way off – the road
was so straight and he had arrived early. He stood shivering in the
drizzle. She felt sorry, but also a little prideful: it was the prospect
of seeing her body that had raised this big man from his bed. Still, it
590 was a sacrifice, she knew, for her friend to come out to meet her on a
weekday morning. He worked all night long and kept the daytime for

548 **teeter** (v) (here) be
about to fall
560 **cheeky** disrespectful
in a funny or annoying
way
564 **policy** plan of action
575 **penetrating**
['penətreɪtɪŋ] *durch-
dringend*
587 **shiver** ['ʃɪvə] (v) shake
(e. g. because you are
cold)
588 **drizzle** (n) light rain

sleeping. She watched him waving at her from their agreed meeting spot, just on the corner, in front of the Embassy of Cambodia. After a while, he stopped waving – because she was still so far away – and
595 then, a little later, he began waving again. She waved back, and when she finally reached him they surprised each other by holding hands. 'I'm an excellent badminton player,' Andrew said, as they passed the Embassy of Cambodia. 'I would make you weep for mercy! Next time, instead of swimming we should play badminton somewhere.' Next
600 time, we should go to Paris. Next time, we should go to the moon. He was a dreamer. But there are worse things, Fatou thought, than being a dreamer.

0–20
'So you're a guest and this is your guest?' the girl behind the desk
605 asked.

'I am a guest and this is another guest,' Fatou replied.

'Yeah … that's not really how it works?'

'Please,' Fatou said. 'We've come from a long way.'

'I appreciate that,' the girl said. 'But I really shouldn't let you in, to
610 be honest.'

'Please,' Fatou said again. She could think of no other argument.

The girl took out a pen and made a mark on Fatou's guest pass.

'This one time. Don't tell no one I did this, please. One time only! I'll need to cross off two separate visits.'

615 For one time only, then, Andrew and Fatou approached the changing rooms together and parted at the doors that led to the men's and the women's. In her changing room, Fatou got ready with lightning speed. Yet somehow he was already there on a lounger when she came out, eyes trained on the women's changing room door, waiting for her to
620 emerge.

'Man, this is the life!' he said, putting his arms behind his head.

'Are you getting in?' Fatou asked, and tried to place her hands, casually, in front of her groin.

'Not yet, man, I'm just taking it all
625 in, taking it all in. You go in. I'll come in a moment.'

Fatou climbed down the steps and began to swim. Not elegant, not especially fast, but consistent and
630 determined. Every now and then she would angle her head to try to see if Andrew was still on his chair, smiling to himself. After twenty laps, she swam to where he lay and put her
635 elbows on the tiles.

623 **groin** *Leistengegend*

'You're not coming in? It's so warm. Like a bath.'

'Sure, sure,' he said. 'I'll try it.'

As he sat up his stomach folded in on itself, and Fatou wondered whether he had spent all that time on the lounger to avoid her seeing
640 its precise bulk and wobble. He came toward the stairs; Fatou held out a hand to him, but he pushed it away. He made his way down and stood in the shallow end, splashing water over his shoulders like a prince fanning himself, and then crouching down into it.

'It is warm! Very nice. This is the life, man! You go, swim – I'll follow
645 you.'

Fatou kicked off, creating so much splash that she heard someone in the adjacent lane complain. At the wall, she turned and looked for Andrew. His method, such as it was, involved dipping deep under the water and hanging there like a hippo, then batting his arms till
650 he crested for air, and then diving down again and hanging. It was a lot of energy to expend on such a short distance, and by the time he reached the wall he was panting like a maniac. His eyes – he had no goggles – were painfully red.

'It's O.K.,' Fatou said, trying to take his hand again. 'If you let me,
655 I'll show you how.' But he shrugged her off, and rubbed at his eyes.

'There's too much bloody chlorine in this pool.'

'You want to leave?'

Andrew turned back to look at Fatou. His eyes were streaming. He looked, to Fatou, like a little boy trying to disguise the fact he had been
660 crying. But then he held her hand, under the water.

'No. I'm just going to take it easy right here.'

'O.K.,' Fatou said.

'You swim. You're good. You swim.'

'O.K.,' Fatou said, and set off, and found that each lap was more
665 distracted and rhythmless than the last. She was not used to being watched while she swam. Ten laps later, she suddenly stood up halfway down the lane and walked the rest of the distance to the wall.

'You want to go in the Jacuzzi?' she asked him, pointing to it. In the hot tub sat a woman dressed in a soaking tracksuit, her head covered
670 with a head scarf. A man next to the woman, perhaps her husband, stared at Fatou and said something to her. He was so hairy he was almost as covered as she was. Together they rose up out of the water and left. He was wearing the tiniest of Speedos, the kind Fatou had feared Andrew might wear, and was grateful he had not. Andrew's
675 shorts were perfectly nice, knee length, red and solid, and looked good against his skin.

'No,' Andrew said. 'It's great just to be here with you, watching the world go by.'

640 **bulk** largeness
wobble ['wɒbl] move-
ment from side to side
647 **adjacent** [ə'dʒeɪsnt]
next to sth.
650 **crest** (v) (here) come
up
652 **pant** (v) breathe
heavily
653 **goggles** (pl) tight-
fitting glasses used
when swimming
673 **Speedos** (pl) very
tight type of swim-
ming trunks for males,
named after the swim-
wear brand Speedo

0–21

That same evening, Fatou was fired. Not for the guest passes – the
680 Derawals never found out how many miles Fatou had travelled on
their membership. In fact, it was hard for Fatou to understand exactly
why she was being fired, as Mrs. Derawal herself did not seem able to
explain it very precisely.

'What you don't understand is that we have no need for a nanny,'
685 she said, standing in the doorway of Fatou's room – there was not
really enough space in there for two people to stand without one of
them being practically on the bed. 'The children are grown. We need
a housekeeper, one who cleans properly. These days, you care more
about the children than the cleaning,' Mrs. Derawal added, though
690 Fatou had never cared for the children, not even slightly. 'And that is
of no use to us.'

Fatou said nothing. She was thinking that she did not have a proper
suitcase and would have to take her things from Mrs. Derawal's house
in plastic bags.

695 'And so you will want to find somewhere else to live as soon as
possible,' Mrs. Derawal said. 'My husband's cousin is coming to stay in
this room on Friday – this Friday.'

Fatou thought about that for a moment. Then she said, 'Can I please
use the phone for one call?' Mrs. Derawal inspected a piece of wood
700 that had flaked from the doorframe. But she nodded.

'And I would like to have my passport, please.'

'Excuse me?'

'My passport, please.'

At last Mrs. Derawal looked at Fatou, right into her eyes, but her
705 face was twisted, as if Fatou had just reached over and slapped her.
Anyone could see the Devil had climbed inside poor Mrs. Derawal. He
was lighting her up with a pure fury.

'For goodness' sake, girl, I don't have your passport! What would
I want with your passport? It's probably in a drawer in the kitchen
710 somewhere. Is that my job now, too, to look for your things?'

Fatou was left alone. She packed her things into the decoy shopping
bags she usually took to the swimming pool. While she was doing
this, someone pushed her passport under the door. An hour later, she
carried her bags downstairs and went directly to the phone in the hall.
715 Faizul walked by and lifted his hand for a high-five. Fatou ignored him
and dialled Andrew's number. From her friend's voice she knew that
she had woken him, but he was not even the slightest bit angry. He
listened to all she had to say and seemed to understand, too, without
her having to say so, that at this moment she could not speak freely.
720 After she had said her part, he asked a few quick technical questions
and then explained clearly and carefully what was to happen.

680 **how many miles Fatou had travelled on their membership** how much Fatou used their membership

700 **flake from sth.** *von etwas abblättern*

711 **decoy** ['diːkɔɪ] *(hier) Tarnung*

'It will all be O.K. They need cleaners in my offices – I will ask for you. In the meantime, you come here. We'll sleep in shifts. You can trust me. I respect you, Fatou.'

725 But she did not have her Oyster Card; it was in the kitchen, on the fridge under a magnet of Florida, and she would rather die than go in there. Fine: he could meet her at 6 p.m., at the Brondesbury Overground station. Fatou looked at the grandfather clock in front of her: she had four hours to kill.

730 'Six o' clock,' she repeated. She put the phone down, took the rest of the guest passes from the drawer of the Louis XVI console, and left the house.

'Weighed down a bit today,' the girl at the desk of the health club said, nodding at Fatou's collection of plastic bags. Fatou held out a 735 guest pass for a stamp and did not smile. 'See you next time,' this same girl said, an hour and a half later, as Fatou strode past, still weighed down and still unwilling to be grateful for past favors. Gratitude was just another kind of servitude. Better to make your own arrangements.

Walking out into the cold gray, Fatou felt a sense of brightness, 740 of being washed clean, that neither the weather nor her new circumstance could dim. Still, her limbs were weary and her hair was wet; she would probably catch a cold, waiting out here. It was only four-thirty. She put her bags on the pavement and sat down next to them, just by the bus stop opposite the Embassy of Cambodia. Buses came and went, 745 slowing down for her and then jerking forward when they realized that she had no interest in getting up and on. Many of us walked past her that afternoon, or spotted her as we rode the bus, or through the windscreens of our cars, or from our balconies. Naturally, we wondered what this girl was doing, sitting on damp pavement in the middle of 750 the day. We worried for her. We tend to assume the worst, here in Willesden. We watched her watching the shuttlecock. Pock, smash.

Pock, smash. As if one player could imagine only a violent conclusion and the other only a hopeful return.

From: The New Yorker, *February 11 & 18, 2013, pp. 88–98. – © Zadie Smith 2013.*

736 **stride (strode – stridden)** walk
737 **gratitude** thankfulness
738 **servitude** [ˈsɜːvɪtjuːd] *Knechtschaft*
741 **limb** arm and/or leg
weary [ˈwɪəri] tired
743 **pavement** (BE) = sidewalk (AE) section at the side of the road for people to walk on

51

Info Zadie Smith

Zadie Smith was born in Willesden in Northwest London in 1975. She is the daughter of an English father and a Jamaican mother, who came to Britain in 1969. She graduated from Cambridge University and has taught at several universities. Her first novel, *White Teeth*, and other novels won her many awards. She is Professor of Creative Writing at New York University. She is also a Fellow of the Royal Society of Literature. She lives in London and New York with her husband and two children.

5

C2 A migration journey

Comprehension

1 Complete the following sentences about Fatou's journey using information from the text:

Fatou's home country is **(a)** _____.

When she first left her home, she went to **(b)** _____ with

(c) _____. She lived in the city of **(d)** _____.

There she worked as a **(e)** _____ in a

(f) _____. From there she travelled to

(g) _____ and then on to **(h)** _____, where she

worked as a **(i)** _____ in a **(j)** _____.

She eventually left Italy and arrived in **(k)** _____. There

she has been working for an 'oriental' **(l)** _____. They are

probably from Pakistan or an Arabic country and own several

(m) _____.

C3 'New Person and Old Person'

Look back at sections 0–01 to 0–11 of Smith's story 'The Embassy of Cambodia' and complete tasks 1–5.

Comprehension

1 Examine the following characters from the story. Complete the table below using information from the text:

Character	Social status / employment
Fatou	
Andrew	
The Derawals	

2 Read the narrator's descriptions of the neighbourhood again in sections 0–1, 0–3 and 0–6. Describe the neighbourhood, its buildings and its citizens in your own words.

3 a Do some research on the internet about the Khmer Rouge and their role in Cambodia's historical development in the 20th century.

   b Using this information, explain why the narrator makes the following statement:

'I doubt there is a man or woman among us, for example, who – upon passing the Embassy of Cambodia for the first time – did not immediately think: "genocide."' (ll. 63–65)

The Cambodian Genocide memorial to the Khmer Rouge atrocities located in Wat Somrong Knong, Cambodia

Analysis

4 Refer back to your findings from **3**. List some of the parallels you see between Cambodia's history and Fatou's biography.

5 **Writing** There are two narrators or voices in the text. Write a comparison of the narrations. Which sections have which narrator? Use the categories in the info box (→ Info box, p. 54) to write your text.

Info Narrators and narrations

Every story or novel has a **narrator**, who can either be a character directly involved in the events described in the story, someone observing them from a distance or someone not involved at all.

A **first-person** (singular) **narrator** ('I …') is easy to identify with and usually more personal.

5 A **first-person plural narrator** speaks for two or more people, including him-/herself and sometimes the reader ('we …'). **Second-person narrators** address the reader directly ('you …'). A **third-person narrator** describes events by talking like an outside observer. **Omniscient narrators** know everything, even future events or the thoughts of the characters. **Limited narrators**, on the other hand, have only limited knowledge of the

10 events and their background. A narrator can be **objective** or **subjective** (selective), and even an **unreliable narrator** who is dishonest to the reader. Sometimes unreliable narrators even admit that they cannot be trusted or that they contradict themselves.

C4 The turning point

Look back at the second half of Smith's story 'The Embassy of Cambodia' (sections 0–12 to 0–21) and complete tasks 1–9.

Comprehension

1 Summarize the events in sections 0–12, 0–17 and 0–21 in your own words.

2 Refer back to the information about Cambodia you found in **C3**, **3**. Compare the information you researched with what is written in sections 0–13 and 0–18.

Analysis

3 Writing Analyse the behaviour of the family members after Fatou has saved Asma's life.

4 What do we learn about the narrator? Why could he or she be in a dressing gown in the middle of the day? Check the last paragraph of section 0–13 for information.

5 Fatou is faced with experiences of suffering and evil, or, as she calls it, the 'Devil'. Look at these quotes from the text. Explain briefly what they refer to or what context they come from.

a

> [Andrew]: 'Tell me, why would God choose us especially for suffering when we, above all others, praise his name?' [...]
> 'But it's not him,' Fatou said quietly, looking over Andrew's shoulder at the rain beating the window. 'It's the Devil.'
> (ll. 315–320)

b 'But the Devil was waiting. [...] That was when she knew that the Devil was stupid as well as evil.' (ll. 457–467)

c 'Don't give the Devil your anger, it is his food,' Andrew had said to her, when they first met, a year ago.' (ll. 470–471)

d 'At last Mrs. Derawal looked at Fatou, right into her eyes, but her face was twisted, as if Fatou had just reached over and slapped her. Anyone could see the Devil had climbed inside poor Mrs. Derawal. He was lighting her up with a pure fury.' (ll. 704–707)

6 a What similarities are there between watching a badminton game from outside the embassy walls and observing life to try to make sense of it? Look especially at the last five lines of the story to explain this. Make notes in the table below.

Observing badminton	Observing life

b Why do you think the author decided to divide the story into chapters that look like the score of a badminton match (0–1, 0–2 ...)?

7 Is the ending a positive or a negative one? Can we as readers be optimistic about Fatou's future?

8 a Analyse the role of the embassy in the short story. Why is it important? What does it represent? Write some notes.

   b Speaking Present your analysis to the class.

Motif of the Cambodian flag

Beyond the text

9 Writing Fatou writes a diary entry after she has left the house. Write this entry. Make sure to include her emotions and her interpretation of the events.

C5 Modern slavery?

1 a How would you define the word 'slavery'? Has its definition evolved throughout history?

   b Make a list of rights that people living in slavery do not have.

Analysis

2 In section 0–7 of 'The Embassy of Cambodia' Fatou, the main character, reflects on the question of modern slavery and her own situation. With a partner, discuss how Fatou is treated in the Derawal family's house. Why is this not a normal form of employment?

3 Comment on the Fatou's state of mind at the end of section 0–7: 'No, on balance she did not think she was a slave.' (ll. 180–181)

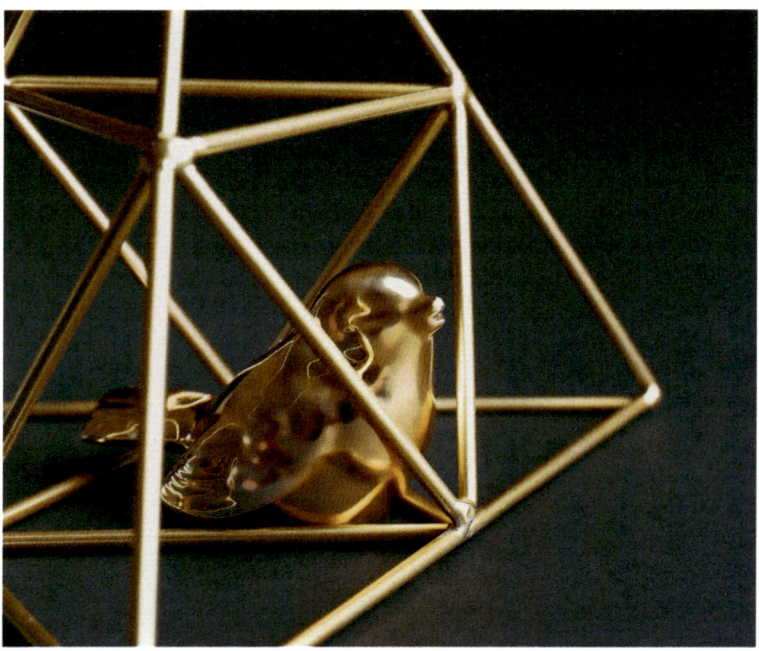

Info Modern slavery

When one thinks of **slavery**, the first images that usually come to mind are from decades ago. However, even today some people still live in slavery or under slavery-like conditions throughout the world. This text by the UN Voluntary Trust Fund on Contemporary Forms of Slavery names some of the forms modern-day slavery can have.

Today numerous contemporary manifestations of slavery affect millions of people across the world. The UN Slavery Fund works to assist the victims of these atrocious practices, which
5 include among others:

Traditional slavery – individuals are born into slavery and are ascribed a slave status which lasts for life. They are, in effect, the property of the families who control them.

10 **Debt bondage** – a person is held as collateral against a loan. The work of the bonded labourer is the means of repaying the loan. Since such labourers receive little or no pay, loan repayment is difficult, and his or her debt may
15 even be inherited by the next generation.

Serfdom – a form of servile labour that binds a person by law, custom or agreement to work on land that belongs to someone else. The labourer's inability to change status makes this
20 a form of slavery.

Forced labour – work that is exacted under coercion, force, penalty, threats, intimidation and the denial of freedom.

Sale of children and worst forms of child labour – include situations of child labour which are characterised by slavery, sexual exploitation, illicit activities and hazardous
25 work that is likely to harm the health, safety or morale of children. […]

From: United Nations Voluntary Trust Fund on Contemporary Forms of Slavery: The Human Faces of Slavery.
https://www.ohchr.org/Documents/Issues/Slavery/UNVTCFS/UNSlaveryFund.pdf

Post-reading activities

Part A
Reviewing colonial and post-colonial challenges

A1 A colonial experience: 'An Outpost of Progress' *Joseph Conrad*

In Joseph Conrad's short story 'An Outpost of Progress', a trading company sends two incompetent employees, Kayerts and Carlier, to a remote trading post in Congo. Read the following excerpt from the text and complete the tasks that follow on p. 60.

Carlier said one evening, waving his hand about, 'In a hundred years, there will be perhaps a town here. Quays, and warehouses, and barracks, and – and – billiard-rooms. Civilization, my boy, and virtue – and all. And then, chaps will read that two good fellows, Kayerts and
5   Carlier, were the first civilized men to live in this very spot!' [...]

2 **quay** [kiː] platform to board, load or unload ships
3 **virtue** [ˈvɜːtʃuː] morally good behaviour
4 **chap** (infml, BE) guy, man

On the ground before the door of the fetish lay six splendid tusks.
'What did you give for it?' asked Kayerts, after surveying the lot
with satisfaction.

'No regular trade,' said Makola. 'They brought the ivory and gave it
10 to me. I told them to take what they most wanted in the station. It is
a beautiful lot. No station can show such tusks. Those traders wanted
carriers badly, and our men were no good here. No trade, no entry in
books: all correct.'

Kayerts nearly burst with indignation. 'Why!' he shouted, 'I believe
15 you have sold our men for these tusks!' Makola stood impassive and
silent. 'I – I – will – I,' stuttered Kayerts. 'You fiend!' he yelled out.

'I did the best for you and the Company,' said Makola, imperturbably.
'Why you shout so much? Look at this tusk.'

'I dismiss you! I will report you – I won't look at the tusk. I forbid
20 you to touch them. I order you to throw them into the river. You – you!'

'You very red, Mr. Kayerts. If you are so irritable in the sun, you
will get fever and die – like the first chief!' pronounced Makola impressively. [...]

Carlier came back on the verandah. 'They're all gone, hey?' asked
Kayerts from the far end of the common room in a muffled voice. 'You
25 did not find anybody?'

'Oh, yes,' said Carlier, 'I found one of Gobila's people lying dead
before the huts – shot through the body. We heard that shot last night.'

Kayerts came out quickly. He found his companion staring grimly
over the yard at the tusks, away by the store. They both sat in silence
30 for a while. Then Kayerts related his conversation with Makola. Carlier
said nothing. At the midday meal they ate very little. They hardly
exchanged a word that day. A great silence seemed to lie heavily over
the station and press on their lips. Makola did not open the store; he
spent the day playing with his children. He lay full-length on a mat
35 outside his door, and the youngsters sat on his chest and clambered
all over him. It was a touching picture. Mrs. Makola was busy cooking
all day, as usual. The white men made a somewhat better meal in the
evening. Afterwards, Carlier smoking his pipe strolled over to the store;
he stood for a long time over the tusks, touched one or two with his
40 foot, even tried to lift the largest one by its small end. He came back
to his chief, who had not stirred from the verandah, threw himself in
the chair and said –

'I can see it! They were pounced upon while they slept heavily after
drinking all that palm wine you've allowed Makola to give them. A
45 put-up job! See? The worst is, some of Gobila's people were there, and
got carried off too, no doubt. The least drunk woke up, and got shot for
his sobriety. This is a funny country. What will you do now?'

'We can't touch it, of course,' said Kayerts.

'Of course not,' assented Carlier.

6 **tusk** long, curved tooth that pokes out of an elephant's mouth
14 **indignation** outrage
16 **fiend** [fiːnd] unfriendly, evil person
17 **imperturbable** [ˌɪmpəˈtɜːbəbl] undisturbed, calm
24 **muffled** *gedämpft*
35 **clamber** [ˈklæmbə] (v) climb with difficulty
41 **stir** (v) (here) move
43 **pounce on sb.** jump on sb. to attack them
45 **put-up job** *abgekartetes Spiel*
49 **assent to sth./sb.** [əˈsent] agree with sth./sb.

50 'Slavery is an awful thing,' stammered out Kayerts in an unsteady voice.

'Frightful – the sufferings,' grunted Carlier with conviction.

They believed their words. Everybody shows a respectful deference to certain sounds that he and his fellows can make. But about feelings 55 people really know nothing. We talk with indignation or enthusiasm; we talk about oppression, cruelty, crime, devotion, self-sacrifice, virtue, and we know nothing real beyond the words. Nobody knows what suffering or sacrifice mean – except, perhaps the victims of the mysterious purpose of these illusions.

60 Next morning they saw Makola very busy setting up in the yard the big scales used for weighing ivory. [...] Carlier said to Kayerts in a careless tone: 'I say, chief, I might just as well give him a lift with this lot into the store.'

As they were going back to the house Kayerts observed with a sigh: 65 'It had to be done.' And Carlier said: 'It's deplorable, but, the men being Company's men the ivory is Company's ivory. We must look after it.'

From: Korff und Ringel-Eichinger. One Language Many Voices, pp.18; 25–28. Cornelsen: 2009.

53 deference
['defərəns] respect for sb./sth.
56 devotion dedication, commitment
65 deplorable
[dɪ'plɔːrəbl] regrettable

Comprehension
1 Describe how Kayerts and Carlier perceive their role in the first paragraph.
2 Outline the elements of the deal between Makola and the traders.
3 Describe how Makola and the two Europeans behave in the aftermath of the dreadful night.

Analysis
4 Examine the language (→ Info box, p. 32) Kayerts and Carlier use and how they express their disapproval of Makola's secret deal.
5 Compare Makola to Kayerts and Carlier and explain why the two Europeans are only formally in charge of the trading post.

Beyond the text
6 YOU CHOOSE
  a Writing Write Kayerts's diary entry two days after the nightly incident.
  OR
  b Speaking Act out a dialogue between Makola and a friend in which he brags about his successful deal.
7 Comment on the title of the story and discuss the ways in which Joseph Conrad criticizes colonialism in his short story.

A2 The London bombings on 7 July 2005

Read the following newspaper blurbs and complete the tasks that follow on pp. 62–63.

On July 7, 2005, four suicide bombers targeted London's transport network at the height of morning rush hour. Backpack bombs were detonated on three underground trains and a bus. Fifty-two people were killed and more than 700 were injured. [...]

5   John Falding's partner, Anat Rosenberg, was killed that morning when one of the bombers blew himself up on a double-decker bus. [...]

    And so we lay on the bed and just cuddled, and I held her for a quarter of an hour. That quarter of an hour, that quarter of an

10 hour, that cuddle, really killed her. Because she left at 9 o'clock instead of a quarter to 9. If she'd left at the usual time, she would've missed the bomb.

From: Rich Presto, Ari, Sharipo, The Painful memories of Those Who Survived London's 2005 Terror Attacks, *National Public Radio, 7 July 2015*

The bombers' journey began at 04:00 BST as three of the group – Mohammad Sidique Khan, 30, Shehzad Tanweer, 22, and 18-year-old Hasib Hussain – left Leeds, West Yorkshire, in a rented car bound for Luton, Bedfordshire. There they met their

5 fourth accomplice, 19-year-old Germaine Lindsay, before heading to the capital by train.

    They went on to detonate four devices – three on the Underground and one on a double-decker bus.

[1] **BST** British Standard Time

From: 7 July London Bombings: What Happened That Day? BBC News, *3 July 2015*

In one sense the meaning of 7/7 is as clear to Britons as that of 9/11 is to Americans. It was a savage, brutal attack intended to sow mayhem and terror. Yet whereas 9/11 was the work of a foreign terrorist group, 7/7 was the work of British citizens. The question

5 that haunts London, but that Washington has so far barely had to face, is why four men brought up in Britain were gripped by such fanatic zeal for a murderous, medieval dogma. [...]

    Many second-generation British Muslims now find themselves detached from both the religious traditions of their parents, which

10 they often reject, and the wider secular society that insists on viewing them simply as Muslims. A few are drawn inevitably to extremist Islamist groups where they discover a sense of identity and of belonging. It is this that has made them open to radicalization.

[2] **savage** ['sævɪdʒ] (n) (here) person who is uncivilized and violent
[3] **mayhem** chaos
[5] **haunt sb./sth.** (v) (here) trouble sb./sth.
[7] **zeal** eagerness, enthusiasm
[9] **detached** (here) disconnected

From: Kenan Malik, Assimilation's Failure, Terrorism's Rise, The New York Times, *6 July 2020*

[London's mayor, Sadiq Khan]: 'The way that our city responded and stood united in the aftermath of the attack showed the world that our values of decency, tolerance and mutual respect will always overcome the hate of the terrorists.'

[3] **decency** ['diːsnsi] respectful behaviour
mutual ['mjuːtʃuəl] *gegenseitig*

From: 7/7 London Bombings: Mayor Pays Tributes to Victims, *BBC News, 7 July 2020*

Comprehension

1 Decide whether the following statements are true (T) or false (F) by ticking the box. If the statement is false, correct it in the space provided.

Statement	T	F
A Four suicide bombers killed 52 people in a dreadful attack in London. Correction: _____ _____	○	○
B Anat Rosenberg was killed because she took an earlier train. Correction: _____ _____	○	○
C The three terrorists travelled to London where they planted bombs in a rental car and a double-decker bus. Correction: _____ _____	○	○
D The terrorists were immigrants from Jamaica. Correction: _____ _____	○	○
E Many second-generation immigrants feel rootless, which makes them susceptible to radicalization. Correction: _____ _____	○	○
F London's mayor, Sadiq Khan, vowed that terrorists would never succeed in shattering the nation's solidarity. Correction: _____ _____	○	○

Analysis

2 Examine the choice of words in the news excerpts. (→ Info box, p. 32). How are they used to express the horror of the attacks?

3 Point out possible causes for the aggression.

Beyond the text

4 a Think: Come up with the three most important challenges immigrants are facing and how to tackle them.

   b Pair: Compare your ideas with a partner.

   c Share: `Speaking` Present your findings to the class.

A3 A multicultural experience: 'A Pair of Jeans' *Qaisra Shahraz*

In this excerpt from the short story 'A Pair of Jeans', a second-generation immigrant, Miriam, lives a double life caught between the traditional culture of her parents and the modern British life she has grown up with. She is engaged to her fiancé, Farook, whose parents, Ayub and Begum, are visiting. When Miriam returns home, they have already arrived and see her wearing Western clothes. Read the following excerpt from the text and complete the tasks that follow on p. 64.

'Deny it as much as you like, Miriam,' her heart whispered back. 'It's no use. They have seen another side of you – your other persona.'

   The other 'persona' had apparently, by either sheer accident or mere contrivance, remained hidden from them from the very beginning.
5 When they first saw her at a party, she was dressed in a maroon chiffon sari and later on each occasion she was always smartly but discreetly and respectably dressed in a traditional shalwar kameze suit. Never at any time had they glimpsed a jean-clad Miriam with an inch of midriff showing! In fact, judging by her mother's expression and lack
10 of composure, it must have been a nasty shock! For now, they were seeing her as a young college woman who was very much under the sway of Western fashion and by extension its moral values. Muslim girls do not go outdoors dressed like that, especially in the short jacket, which hardly covered her hips and a skimpy vest. She had heard of
15 stories about in-laws who were prejudiced against such girls. For they weren't the docile, the obedient and sweet daughter-in-laws that they preferred. On the contrary, they were seen as a threat and portrayed as rebellious *hoydens*, who did not respect either their husbands or their in-laws. Miriam was all too familiar with such stereotyped views
20 of women. [...]

   [Ayub]: 'Well, what do you think of your future daughter-in-law? I thought you told me she was a very "sharif", a very modest girl. Was that naked waist what you would call modest? He lanced at her. [...]

4 contrivance
[kən'traɪvəns]
(fml) clever plan
5 maroon [mə'ru:n]
brownish red colour
chiffon ['ʃɪfɒn] type
of material you can see
through, usually for
clothing
6 sari ['sɑːri] long traditional cloth worn
around the body, esp.
worn by women in
South Asia
7 shalwar kameez
[ʃʌl'wɑː kə'miːz] tradi-
tional dress
8 glimpse sth. (v) see
sth.
9 midriff ['- -] waist
12 sway (n) power,
influence
14 skimpy (here) small,
not covering much of
the body
16 docile ['dəʊsaɪl]
well-behaved and
obedient
18 hoyden wild girl
23 lance at sb. (v) (here)
attack sb. verbally

'Tell me, in those clothes of hers, would you be proud to have her
25 as your daughter-in-law? I know I am not. You talk about her being
a university student. Well, have you any idea what sort of company
that she might be keeping with that lot. You've only seen her at odd
times, and always at home. Do you know what she is really like? Have
you thought of the effect she could have in your household? With
30 her lifestyle, such girls also want a lot of freedom. In fact, they want
to lead their lives the way their English college friends do. Did you
notice what time she came in? She knew we were coming, yet that had
not made any difference to her lifestyle. So you expect her to change
overnight to suit us? People form habits, Begum, do you understand?
35 Are you prepared for a daughter-in-law who goes in and out of the
house whenever she feels like it, dressed like that and returns home as
late as that? Don't your cheeks burn at the thought of that bit of flesh
you saw? Imagine how our son will feel about her! I hope shame! And
what if she has a boyfriend already – have you thought of that? What
40 if she has a boyfriend already? What if she takes drugs? What if …
What if … So many questions to ask ourselves! Do you know, we do
not know this girl at all, Begum! Can you guarantee that she will make
our son happy?'

From: 'A Pair of Jeans'. In: Korff und Ringel-Eichinger. One Language Many Voices,
pp. 178; 182–183, Cornelsen: 2009.

Comprehension
1 Describe Miriam's expectations.
2 Outline her future in-laws' fears.

Analysis
3 Illustrate Ayub's view of British society.

Beyond the text
4 a With a partner, prepare a dialogue in which Ayub challenges a
British neighbour's view of society.
  b Speaking Act out your dialogue.
5 Discuss the role of arranged marriage in different societies.